FILM FINANCE
FOR BEGINNERS

FILM FINANCE FOR BEGINNERS

By
Jeffrey Taylor

Copyright © 2010
By Jeffrey Taylor

All rights reserved. No part of this book may be used or reproduced without prior written permission (except in the case of brief quotation embodied in reviews.)

To order your own personal copy please visit

http://filmfinanceforbeginners.com

or

http://booksbyjeffreytaylor.com

First Edition, December 2010

Taylor, Jeffrey
Film Finance For Beginners

0-9727047-5-2

1. Taylor, Jeffrey
2. Film Finance
3. Independent Film Finance
4. Title

OTHER BOOKS BY JEFFREY TAYLOR

Selling Leasing In A Tough Economy

The Future of Equipment Leasing

A Gentleman Drunk/Un Caballero Borracho

Going From W2 to 1099

Acknowledgments

Over the years, I have met hundreds of writers, actors, directors, producers, distributors, photographers, makeup artists and financiers. I would like to single out the rare few who have shared personal experiences with me so that I could write a better book.

Lorri Allen
Don Baillargeon
David Balsiger
Jon Bonnell
Ted Chalmers
Chuck Foster
Steve Harrison
Chris Hazel
Jordana Hazel
David Kidder
Mary Ann Mercer
Larry Stouffer
Moira Taylor

My very special love to Toby who tolerates my going on the computer at 2:00 am to do my research.

Additional thanks to the people who helped me put together this book.

Martin Coffee
Sage Evans

Contents

Acknowledgments vii
Introduction ix
Evolution of the Major Studios 17
The History of Independent Film 39
The African Queen 49
The Production Code of 1930 57
Getting the Public to See Your Movie 63
Learn to Become a Producer.. 69
Prepare to Meet Your Investor 77
Managing Investor Attitudes... 93
Basic Accounting Terms 99
Preparing Budgets 105
Hollywood Accounting 121
What Makes a Great Movie? 129
Isolating Investment Risk Through
     Limited Liability Corporations (LLCs) 135
What Makes a Great Business Plan? 141
Financing Alternatives 157
Film Distribution... 165
Film Tax Incentives 171
"The Internet Threat" 185
Summary 193

Introduction

Let's assume that you have a great script, know many people in the film industry, and still can't your project off the ground. What can you do about it? What's stopping you from going to the next level?

If you are like most aspiring moviemakers, you have produced your promos/trailers, worked the film festival circuit, attended film finance conferences and talked to anyone who will listen to you -- and many people have shown a tremendous amount of interest. Yet, they do not want to put their own money into your film or do not want to open the door to people who might be willing to put money into your project.

When I started financing independent films, I relied on moviemakers to present me with terms and conditions, which I could not validate in the market. As a result, I did not know if the deal was good or not. In many cases, I did not get good deals. In fact, I lost a lot of money.

To date I have financed several independent films and one dinner theater. None of them has made a lot of money. Do I consider that a failure? Absolutely not. My dad always told me, "You'll have more losers in life than winners." However, to stay in business, your winners have to cover the losses from your losers. As a result, I am able to continue financing films, and still hope to hit the jackpot.

Independent moviemakers do not fail because they make bad movies; they fail because either they run out of money during the film production process or they fail to raise enough money to cover their costs to market their movie appropriately and effectively. In either case, the independent moviemaker fails to develop a long-term strategy that allows him to make movies as a life-long career.

Think of a homebuilder who builds a house with his own money, but fails to convince a bank to provide him with a construction or home equity loan. Even if he completes the house, he may not have enough money to furnish it. Even if the homebuilder has enough money to furnish the house, he may not have enough money to properly market the property. And, on top of that, even if he has the money to market his well-crafted, beautifully designed 5-bedroom luxury home, he may not be able to find a buyer willing to pay his price. A similar situation faces all independent moviemakers.

Many people think that they have what it takes to make a movie. From early childhood, we are enchanted by the idea of making movies. We sat in front of the TV as a kid, went to the movies, and watched cartoons. Many of us dream about making movies, but we fail to make our dreams a reality. For the few of us who dare to make a movie, we fail to learn how to do it sensibly and with a coherent strategy.

Many independent moviemakers focus on loglines, story summaries, plots, action, dialogue and surprise elements. They focus on their once-in-a-lifetime script, and peddle it as a unique creation without thinking about how much it will cost or generate at the box office, DVD store and on the Internet. They rarely focus on the post-production costs, let alone the marketing costs (the true hurdle for a film's financial success). In short, the independent moviemaker underestimates the true cost of making the film. On top of that, they rarely talk intelligently to investors, because the independent moviemaker does not learn the unique terms and language used by sophisticated investors.

Many independent filmmakers spend an inordinate amount of time lining up talent and actors with high name recognition. In the process, the filmmaker loses track of the financial side of the equation and never hooks the investors. In fact, many movies do not get made, because the screenwriter and/or producer tries to attach actors who need to see the money first, while investors will simply not put up the money unless the actor is available and committed to the project. This most ubiquitous and hated Catch-22 afflicts the majority of independent films.

Does every independent moviemaker have to think like a Wall Street banker? The answer is "no." However, if the moviemaker wants to make movies year after year after year, he/she must build a reputation of profitability. Success does not come from hitting home runs; it comes from hitting singles each and every time one goes to bat.

Is there a way to ensure the profitability of a movie? Yes. However, you have to line up all of the pre-production, production and marketing elements before you start filming.

Let's meet the first-time indie filmmaker. She is young, ambitious and just out of one of the top LA or NY film schools. She has tremendous energy, enthusiasm and a bottomless reservoir of out-of-the-box creativity. She surrounds herself with other creative types yearning to make a breakout film. Instead of trying to hit singles and get on base, she goes for the home run and fails her investors. In other words, the indie filmmaker, and her investors, tried to hit the jackpot in Vegas, win the Powerball lottery, or cash in on an exploding penny stock.

Now meet the first-time accountant. He is young, aloof and graduated from a university with an advanced accounting degree. He has discipline and expert knowledge in accounting, taxes, budgeting and finance. He hangs out with other accounting professionals and shuns the limelight. Secretly, however, he admires the life of the moviemaker, but does not have the courage (or financial wherewithal) to pursue the life of an artist.

What would happen if an indie filmmaker could combine the best parts of these two worlds? What if one could be creative, yet follow the rules of business discipline? Do you think this combination would guarantee financial success year after year after year?

Take a hard look at any other industry (e.g., banking, aircraft manufacturing, waste management, solar). They predict profitability through accurate forecasting and budgeting, and seek to find wholesalers and distributors to sell their products to retail stores and end-users. The problem with indie filmmakers is that they focus too much on the "show" and not enough on the "business." Similarly, if a toy manufacturer created a new toy at a cost that the public would not or could not afford, he would be out of business in a heartbeat.

To make profitable movies, one has to learn more about accounting, taxes, finance, and budgeting, for without them, a filmmaker will never be able to develop a long-term record of producing profitable pictures. And with success comes greater and greater amounts of capital, which brings more and more wealth.

In recent years, many independent films should not have been made. When the stock market, real estate markets and government securities became less and less attractive to qualified investors, financially astute people put a lot of money into poorly made and poorly conceived films, in a vain hope to make up for their other losses. Having produced an oversupply of mediocre movies, it is no wonder that indie filmmakers face indifference, if not outright hostility, from potential investors.

If you plan to court a seasoned and savvy movie investor, you better be damn sure that he is going to review your business plan and movie script against a series of guidelines to determine if your movie can be made and sold for a profit. If the investor is going to provide financing without any form of security other than a promise of success, he is going to do everything possible to ensure the probability of a profit.

When I first started to invest in independent films, there were very few books, articles and seminars on the subject. Lawyers accustomed to making six-figure fees on studio-based projects wrote most of the books, so the level of germane information was scant. There were no courses to explain how to manufacture a movie using accounting rules and financial budgets. Of course, there was plenty of literature on acting, auditioning, filmmaking techniques and the like, but that didn't help me, as a businessperson, judge the potential profitability of a film project.

As an indie film investor, I learned early on that there were only two ways to make money in independent films: 1) generate revenues by looking at alternative uses of the film and 2) reduce production/distribution costs by outsourcing certain key elements.

In fact, most investors never invest in a second film because they had such a negative experience with their first one. Sadly, for the few investors that made money in their first few films, they lose their money after a while because they eventually make bad decisions. Their emotions and ego take over and start to override good solid business judgment and decision-making.

Although it sounds simple, I am quite surprised by the number of independent filmmakers who fail to get their projects produced. You would think that even a novice filmmaker would research the necessary business requirements of making a film before shooting.

I truly believe that any competent moviemaker can make a profitable film. In order to do so, one has to learn the basic rules of movie accounting, taxes, finance and budgeting, and get a committed buyer with cash to market and distribute the film. For without these disciplines, only luck will save you.

As a service to the indie film community, I do not charge for my time. As long as you continue to learn, I will help you. If I think you have a profitable project I will either invest in the project or let my friends know about it. My contact information is located at http://showbizmanagementadvisors.com.

Chapter 1
Evolution of the Major Studios

The first machine that showed animated pictures or motion pictures was a device called the "wheel of life" or "zoopraxiscope." Patented in 1867 by William Lincoln, eager movie watchers saw moving drawings and/or photographs through a slit in a box.

In 1889, the first commercial transparent roll film, perfected by Eastman Kodak, was put on the market. The availability of this flexible film made possible the development of Thomas Edison's motion picture camera in 1891, which enabled one person at a time to view moving pictures.

Meanwhile, in 1891 Louis Lumiére was credited as inventing the first motion picture camera. That same year the Lumiére Brothers were the first to present projected, moving, photographic pictures to a paying audience. What Lumiere invented was a portable motion-picture camera, film processing unit and projector called the Cinematographe — three functions covered in one invention.

A constant flow of new film subjects was needed to keep Edison's new invention popular, so he built a motion picture production studio. In 1893, Edison built the first movie studio in the United States -- the Black Maria, a tarpaper-covered structure near his laboratories in New Jersey and asked circus, vaudeville, and dramatic actors to perform for the camera. Edison distributed these movies at vaudeville theaters, penny arcades, wax museums, and fairgrounds.

Performance acts from Buffalo Bill's Wild West Show were also filmed, including Annie Oakley and a troop of Native American dancers. Many of these films were expected to appeal to male audiences, and so some featured scantily clad women. Other masculine activities, such as boxing and cockfights, were also filmed.

The first Kinetoscope parlor, owned by the Holland Brothers, opened on April 14, 1894, in New York. Five kinetoscope machines were placed in a row and a customer could view the films in each machine for a total of 25 cents. Kinetoscope parlors soon opened around the United States.

In 1886, H. H. Wilcox bought an area of the Rancho La Brea section of Los Angeles that his wife then christened "Hollywood." Within a few years, Wilcox had devised a grid plan for his new community, paved Prospect Avenue (now Hollywood Boulevard) for his main street and sold large residential lots to wealthy Midwesterners looking to build homes so they could "winter in California."

Later in 1896, Edison introduced his improved Vitascope, his first commercially-successful projector in the US, and the dream factory was born.

In the early 1900s, companies started moving to Los Angeles because of the good weather and longer days. Although electric lights were by then widely available, none were yet powerful enough to adequately expose film. Most early silent movies were shot on the roofs of buildings in downtown Los Angeles. Early movie producers also relocated to Southern California to escape Edison's Motion Picture Patents Company, which controlled almost all the patents relevant to movie production at the time.

In 1911, the Nestor Company opened Hollywood's first film studio in an old tavern on the corner of Sunset and Gower. Not long thereafter, Cecil B. DeMille and D. W. Griffith began making movies in the area, as they were drawn to the locale for its vast open space and year-round moderate climate.

The roots of independent film can be traced back to the early pioneer filmmakers who resisted Thomas Edison's egregious monopoly practices. Independent filmmakers built their own cameras and moved to Southern California where they laid the foundations of the American film industry as well as the Hollywood Studio System.

The demands of this thriving new industry created radical changes in the burgeoning community, causing a clash between older and newer residents. Acres of agricultural land south of Hollywood Boulevard was subdivided and developed as housing for newcomers. High-rise commercial buildings began to spring up along Hollywood Boulevard, with development concentrating at Highland, Cahuenga, and Vine. And the super wealthy, who wanted to be in the ritziest of neighborhoods, left Hollywood for the up-and-coming Beverly Hills.

By the mid-1920s, a handful of American production companies had evolved into powerful and cash-laden film industry conglomerates, contracting with performers and filmmaking personnel to work for company owned studios, distributors and theaters.

Five large film companies – 20th Century-Fox, Metro-Goldwyn-Mayer, Paramount, RKO and Warner Brothers – were formed and came to be known as "the Big Five," "Majors," or "the Studios" in trade publications (such as *Variety*).

Although they owned few or no theaters to guarantee sales of their films (which the Big Five did), Universal Pictures, Columbia Pictures and United Artists also fell under this rubric, thus making a total of eight generally recognized "major studios." United Artists has a rich history starting from its founding by Charlie Chaplin, Mary Pickford, D.W. Griffith and Douglas Fairbanks (all top creative talent of the day) in 1919.

Stars powered the American Studio System from 1934-1946. Various studios, such as 20th Century-Fox, Paramount Pictures, Metro-Goldwyn-Mayer, Columbia Pictures and Warner Brothers held long-term performance contracts for both stars and directors.

For example:

20th Century-Fox - Otto Preminger, Elia Kazan, Shirley Temple, Loretta Young, Betty Grable, Marilyn Monroe, Tyrone Power, Don Ameche, Henry Fonda, and Gregory Peck.

Paramount - Mary Pickford, Mae West, W. C. Fields, Bing Crosby, Bob Hope, Gary Cooper, Claudette Colbert, Alan Ladd, Burt Lancaster, and Kirk Douglas.

Metro-Goldwyn-Mayer (MGM) - Greta Garbo, Clark Gable, Joan Crawford, Spencer Tracy, James Stewart, Mickey Rooney, Judy Garland, and Elizabeth Taylor.

Warner Brothers - Humphrey Bogart, Edward G. Robinson, Jimmy Cagney, Bette Davis, Errol Flynn, and Peter Lorre.

Stars weren't free to seek their own employment contracts during these early years. Instead, Stars would be "loaned out" by one studio to another for a particular project. The Studios expected their Stars to churn out 4-5 pictures a year, often working on multiple pictures at the same time.

When the English director Alfred Hitchcock made his first American film, "Rebecca" (1940), he joined the pantheon of famous directors under contract by the American studios. He later switched studios for his 1941 film "Suspicion," which was made for RKO Pictures (Radio-Keith-Orpheum); the same studio that took a gigantic risk by refusing to back down under the campaign waged by newspaper magnate William Randolph Hearst to prevent "Citizen Kane" (1941), directed by Orson Welles, from ever seeing the light of day.

At the dawn of Hollywood and the motion picture industry, the Studios were able to own the actual theaters in which their films played. This was a major source of revenue for the studios and eight independent producers, including Samuel Goldwyn, David O. Selznick and Walt Disney, eventually opposed the Big Five's ownership of movie theaters.

In 1938, the US Government filed a famous lawsuit against the Hollywood Studio System. It reached the Supreme Court (*The United States v. Paramount Pictures, Inc*), and the suit contended that the major studios held an unfair monopoly in controlling production, distribution, and exhibition of films through ownership of their theater chains, thus violating federal anti-trust laws.

In 1948, the US Supreme Court ruled that the vertically integrated structure of the movie industry constituted an illegal monopoly and barred the Studios from continued ownership of their theaters. The Studios were forced to divest from the lucrative exhibition business. This decision, reached after twelve long, hard years of litigation, accelerated the end of the Studio System and Hollywood's "Golden Age."

With the advent and growth of television in the 1950s, the rise of the director as auteur and the ability for actors to become "free agents" the old Studio System was finished. It kicked around for another decade or so, but when that empire crashed, the aftermath was a period of chaos and fertile growth.

The decade of the 1950s was known for many things, including post-war affluence, increased leisure time, the Korean War, the advent of middle-class values, and the rise of modern jazz. Young Americans demanded convenience and that pressure encouraged the creation of 'fast food' restaurants and drive-in movie theaters. Everyone wanted babies, all-electric homes, television, and TV dinners. To ensure that people had money, stores, gasoline stations and banks invented that dubious financial instrument: the credit card.

After WWII, young people wanted new and exciting symbols of rebellion. Hollywood responded to audience demand, and the late 1940s and 1950s saw the rise of the anti-hero -- with stars like exciting newcomers James Dean, Paul Newman, and Marlon Brando.

American Bandstand first began as a local program for teens on WFIL-TV in Philadelphia in early October 1952. In mid-1956, a 26 year-old Dick Clark was the new host chosen for ABC-TV's *American Bandstand*. By the time the show first aired nationally, in mid-1957, it had become a mainstay for rock group performances.

Hollywood soon realized that young affluent teenagers wanted to see movies laced with popular music. "Blackboard Jungle" was the first major Hollywood film to use rock 'n' roll on its soundtrack (*Rock Around the Clock*).

Elvis Presley was featured as an actor in many popular and profitable films after signing his first film deal in

1956. His screen debut was Paramount's Civil War drama "Love Me Tender," which featured a #1 single hit song ballad.

Teens and young adults attended outdoor drive-ins that showed exploitative, cheap fare created especially for them. Producer/director Roger Corman (the 'B-movie King') became known for his low-budget, short, sci-fi/horror quickies. His credits included "Not of This Earth," "Attack of the Crab Monsters," and "The Blob" (which introduced Steve McQueen to the world), "A Bucket of Blood," "The Wasp Woman," and "I Was A Teenage Werewolf."

Theater attendance declined precipitously as free broadcast TV viewing made inroads into the entertainment business. In 1951, NBC became America's first nationwide TV network, and in just a few years, 50% of US homes had at least one TV set. In March of 1953, the Academy Awards were televised for the first time by NBC, and the broadcast received the largest single audience in network TV's five-year history. By 1954, NBC's *Tonight Show* had become one of the most popular late-night TV shows.

With a steep decline in weekly theater attendance, Studios were forced to find creative ways to make money from television. By mid-decade, the major studios began licensing to television the film rights to their pre-1948 films for broadcast. The first feature film to be broadcast on US television, on November 3, 1956, during prime time, was "The Wizard of Oz."

In 1956, the Studios lifted the ban against film stars making TV appearances. The fast-talking, cigar-smoking, and quick-witted Groucho Marx (of the famous Marx Brothers) brought his popular radio show *You Bet Your Life* to NBC as a game show in 1950, which lasted until 1961.

Television (just a small black and white screen) had become affordable and plentiful, so Hollywood moviemakers fought back with gimmicks – extensive use of color film, widescreen exhibition (CinemaScope, VistaVision, 70mm) and 3D. By the mid-1950s, more than half of Hollywood's productions were made in color to lure people out of their homes and back into the theaters.

The cinema of the 1960s reflected the decade of fun, fashion, rock 'n' roll, tremendous social changes (i.e., the Civil Rights era and anti-war marches) and transitional cultural values. This was a turbulent decade of monumental changes, national tragedies, cultural events, assassinations and unexpected deaths, and technological advancements, including the invention of the Barbie Doll, the microchip, TV broadcast in color, touchtone telephones, miniskirts, heart transplants, moon travel and the Arpanet (predecessor to the Internet).

Coincidentally, 1963 was the worst year for US film production in fifty years. With movie audiences declining due to the dominance of television, major American film companies began to diversify with other forms of entertainment: records, publishing, TV movies and the production of TV series.

In September of 1961, *Saturday Night at the Movies* premiered on NBC with the first wide-screen comedy, "How to Marry A Millionaire," marking the start of broadcasting modern Hollywood movies on TV.

Increasingly in the 1960s, the major studios financed and distributed independently produced domestic pictures, and made-for-TV movies became a regular feature of network programming. Many "runaway" film productions were being made in international locales to save money. By the middle of the decade, the average ticket price was less than a dollar, and the average film budget was slightly over $1.5 million. By the end of the decade, the film industry was very depressed and experiencing an all-time low.

Columbia and MGM were forced to sell off their fabled backlots as valuable Southern California real estate (for condominiums and shopping centers). MGM sold various film artifacts in 1970, including Dorothy's ruby slippers from "The Wizard of Oz", offered tours of backlots. Universal began its famed studio tours in 1964. Disney created theme parks (Disney World in Orlando, Florida). The mystery, glamour and mystique of Tinseltown was seriously tarnished and in doubt.

To aid the tourist industry and create another attraction, the Hollywood Chamber of Commerce inaugurated the Hollywood Walk of Fame. The first star, placed on February 9, 1960, was for Joanne Woodward. However, by the mid-1970s, the center of Hollywood was better known for its adult bookstores, prostitutes and dilapidated look.

In 1963, Stanley Durwood became the father of the 'multiplex' movie theater when he opened the first-ever mall multiplex, composed of two side-by-side theaters with 700 seats at Ward Parkway Center in Kansas City. Three years later, Durwood introduced the world's first four-plex and, then in 1969, he built a six-plex with automated projection booths. Durwood went on to head up AMC Entertainment, eventually making it the third-largest movie theater company in the nation.

Due to various financial difficulties, the Studios were quickly taken over by multinational companies looking to expand their portfolio of businesses into entertainment. The traditional Hollywood studio era was over, as unrelated business conglomerates acquired studios to boost their bottom line. As a result, the age of "packaged" films and the independent distribution company and producer was born.

In 1962, the growing entertainment conglomerate MCA (the Music Corporation of America) acquired Universal-International Studios.

In 1966, Gulf+Western Industries bought the floundering Paramount, and under the new, young management of Robert Evans and Peter Bart Paramount became responsible for such influential films as "Rosemary's Baby," "Love Story," "The Godfather," and "Chinatown."

In 1967, Robert Shaye, founded New Line Cinema, as a privately held distributor of art films. Bank of America absorbed United Artists through its Transamerica Corporation subsidiary, and Jack Warner (co-founder of the famous studio) sold his controlling interest in Warner

Bros. to Seven Arts, a Canadian production and distribution corporation.

In 1969, MGM was acquired by the Las Vegas hotel financier and airline mogul Kirk Kerkorian, who won control of the studio in a proxy battle with Seagram's Edgar Bronfman, Sr.

Although the 1970s opened with Hollywood experiencing a financial and artistic depression, the decade was a creative high point in the US film industry; a second Golden Age of Cinema. Restrictions on language, adult content, sexuality, and violence had loosened, and story elements reflected a truer, more realistic portrayal of human drama on the silver screen. Previously, the Studio System had to follow the Production Code of 1930 (described later in the book), but by the late 1960s, Jack Valenti (Hollywood's DC lobbyist) was able to convince Congress that Hollywood could police itself. Thus the Motion Picture Corporation of America was founded and the current ratings system was instituted. In 1969, the first (and only) Rated X film, "Midnight Cowboy," the story of a male prostitute, won Best Picture at the Academy Awards.

The counter-culture of the 1960s had influenced Hollywood to be freer, to take more risks and to experiment with alternative, young filmmakers, as veteran Hollywood professionals and old-style moguls died out and a new generation of filmmakers assumed the reins of control. The 1970s would be noted for films with creative and memorable subject matter that reflected the questioning spirit and truth of the times.

Much of the focus was on box-office receipts and the production of action- and youth-oriented blockbuster films with dazzling special effects. However, it was becoming increasingly more difficult to predict what would sell or become a hit. This was marked on a professional and creative level when "Rocky" (1975) beat out the critically acclaimed "All The President's Men" for Best Picture that year at the Academy Awards. "Rocky" was produced through MGM/United Artist from a script from then unknown and struggling actor Sylvester Stallone, who insisted on playing the titular character.

Hollywood's economic crises in the 1950s and 1960s, especially during the war against the lure of television, were somewhat eased with the emergence in the 1970s of summer "blockbuster" movies or "event films" that were marketed to mass audiences, especially following the awesome success of three influential films: "The Godfather," "Jaws," and "Star Wars." Many people in the Hollywood establishment looked at these three films during the pre-production stages with slight disdain. "The Godfather" starred unknowns and "ugly" people (by Hollywood glamour standards). "Star Wars" was rejected all over town at every major studio – twice. This was beneficial to George Lucas, as he was able to secure commanding control of all over the film's ancillary and merchandising rights. No one thought it was going to do any business.

Although the budget for "Jaws" exploded from $4 million to $9 million during production and threatened to derail Steven Spielberg's burgeoning career, it became the highest grossing film in history - until "Star Wars" came out two years later. Both pictures were the first films to earn more than $100 million in rentals.

Cable television was established in 1972 with the founding of Home Box Office (HBO), the first pay/premium television channel. In 1973, pay cable television allowed profanity and sex far beyond what could be offered on commercial network television – such as profanity-prone George Carlin. Cable TV didn't fall under the authority of the FCC and, therefore, wasn't subject to its restrictive broadcast standard rules and regulations.

In 1975, Michael Ovitz and colleagues (defectors from the stalwart William Morris Agency) founded Creative Artists Agency and became a 'packager' of talent for film projects. The result created intense competition among agencies and ceded huge amounts of industry power to the agents. All the elements of a film were brought together and packaged: screenplay, novel, or stage play combined with proven box-office stars, directors, and marketing strategies. Conglomerates acquired and re-acquired many of the Studios' properties and libraries as part of their leisure entertainment divisions, with decisive power over decisions about which profitable projects were produced.

In 1976, Paramount became the first studio to authorize the release of its film library onto videocassettes with 20th Century-Fox following suit.

In 1977, George Atkinson of Los Angeles began to advertise the rental of 50 magnetic video titles of his own collection in the Los Angeles Times, and launched the first video rental store – Video Station – on Wilshire Boulevard, renting videos for $10/day.

By the end of the decade, the established Hollywood movie studios no longer controlled or dominated production. Although the Studios still maintained a stranglehold on film distribution, independent studios, producers, and/or agents controlled production and financing.

In 1986, the combined share of the six classic majors— at that point Paramount, Warner Bros., Columbia, Universal, Fox, and MGM/UA—fell to 64%, the lowest since the beginning of the Golden Age. Smaller independents garnered 13%.

In the early 1990s, the old, established Studios bounced back. Between 1989 and 1994, Paramount, Warner, Columbia, and Universal all changed ownership in a series of conglomerate purchases and mergers that brought them new financial and marketing muscle. Star salaries and production budgets spiraled into the stratosphere. The most important contenders to emerge during the 1990s – New Line Cinema, the Weinsteins' Miramax, and DreamWorks SKG – were ultimately brought into the majors' fold.

Disney acquired the very successful animation production house Pixar, whose films were distributed by Disney/Buena Vista, in 2006. The development of in-house pseudo-indie subsidiaries by the conglomerates, sparked by the 1992 establishment of Sony Pictures Classics, significantly undermined the position of the true independents.

The major studios released 124 films during 2006. The four largest secondary subsidiaries (Time Warner's New Line, Disney's Miramax, Fox Searchlight, and Universal's Focus Features) accounted for another 46. Box-office domination was fully restored. In 2006, the six major movie conglomerates combined for 91.6% of the North American market.

Until the advent of digital alternatives, the cost of professional film equipment and stock was a major barrier to entry for many would-be players and a huge obstacle to those independent filmmakers who wanted to make their own films. The cost of 35mm film cameras, raw film stock and processing, lighting and post-production costs were out of reach for most low-cost films.

The advent of the personal computer in 1984, consumer camcorders in 1985, the arrival of high-definition digital video in the early 1990s, and non-linear editing software in the late 1990s lowered the technological barrier to movie production considerably. Nowadays, a movie can be made for as low as $50,000, a price within reach of most filmmakers.

On the business side, the cost of big-budget studio films has led to conservative choices which are proven and bankable. They do not take chances when they are fronting investments worth hundreds of millions of dollars. An unproven screenwriter or film director does not get the opportunity to get his or her big break with the Studios, unless he or she otherwise has significant industry experience in film or television. Films with "unknowns" in the cast, particularly in lead roles, are rarely produced by the major studios due to the inherent risk of failure at the box office.

One can blame this on the rise of marketing costs, which can equal or outstrip the actual production costs of the majority of films. Another key expense for independent filmmakers is music. Licensing fees for popular songs can range between US$10,000–$20,000.

The increasing popularity and feasibility of low-budget, high-quality films has led to a vast increase in the number of aspiring filmmakers -- people who have written spec scripts and hope to find several million dollars to turn their scripts into box-office successes.

These aspiring filmmakers often work day jobs while they pitch their scripts to independent film production companies, talent agents, and wealthy investors. Their dream seems much more attainable than before the independent film revolution, because these novice filmmakers no longer need to gain the backing of a major studio with lots of clout and money to realize their dream.

Full-length independent films are often showcased at film festivals, such as Sundance and Cannes. Award winners from these exhibitions are more likely to get picked up for distribution by major film studios, which have the power, money, and connections to get the film into theaters around the world. Unfortunately, not all festival winners get picked up for distribution unless there is already a lot of marketing money behind the project. It is estimated that it costs more than $100,000 just to compete at the Cannes Film Festival.

Ironically, as independent moviemakers make money with their films, major studios continue to falter. In November 2007, major newspapers reported that Tom Cruise, bankrolled with a $500 million check from Wall Street, could not get United Artists back on track.

Its first film, the somber political tale "Lions for Lambs" from acclaimed director Robert Redford, starring Cruise, Redford and Meryl Streep, opened poorly at the box office and never recouped the $35 million investment. Other top box-office disasters at the time from other studios included Oliver Stone's "Alexander" (lost $120 million), the Eddie Murphy vehicle "Pluto Nash" (lost $95 million) and "Speed Racer" (lost $80 million), directed by the successful team behind "The Matrix" movie franchise.

Newspapers reported that Tom Cruise was desperate to save his second movie, "Valkyrie," and questioned his image as a bankable superstar. Hollywood investors were worried about the timing of "Valkyrie's" release -- on Christmas Day. It joined a number of serious but clearly depressing films focusing on either the Holocaust or World War II.

These days an abundance of outside financing for Hollywood movies means that the Studios often don't fully own or control the films they distribute -- an arrangement that limits both their risk and the money they can make, even from a big hit.

For example, Marvel Studios (a unit of Marvel Entertainment) with its own line of credit for movie production owns the wildly successful "Iron Man" franchise, and DreamWorks Animation owns "Kung Fu Panda." This means that most of the film's profits go to the underlying owner, not the film studio that released the film. Paramount, acting as a marketing agent and distributor, received an 8% fee for handling the distribution of "Kung Fu Panda."

Although Paramount and George Lucas jointly own "Indiana Jones and the Kingdom of the Crystal Skull," the lion's share of the profits for the $185 million movie went to Lucas and Spielberg, not Paramount.

Dozens of films are finding there's no room at the local multiplex. The reason: Hollywood is flush with roughly $13 billion to $18 billion in financing for movies that has poured in over the past few years, vastly expanding the number of pictures getting made.

This dynamic has turned movie distribution into a chaotic situation, with too many films vying for too few slots in theaters each weekend. Last year more than 600 feature films - mostly independent movies not produced at a major studio - were released theatrically in the US, up from 466 in 2002, according to the Motion Picture Association of America; that's an average of 9 or more movies every weekend that are battling for the public's attention.

To avoid collisions, the Studios rapidly scaled back the number of films they released, particularly smaller specialty movies. Warner Bros. closed its two art-house labels, Picturehouse and Warner Independent Pictures. Viacom's Paramount Pictures absorbed the majority of the staff at its specialty label, Paramount Vantage, into its main studio and cut about 50 employees.

Major film distributors are far more cautious in acquiring independently financed films for distribution, a situation that has dramatically slowed business at major international film gatherings, including Sundance, Toronto and Cannes.

Look at box-office receipts on any major movie reporting site. Most of the major pictures are making money. According to IMDB, "Shrek 4" crossed the $175 million mark with worldwide gross revenues. Disney's "Prince of Persia: The Sands of Time" starring Jake Gyllenhaal, grossed $56 million.

However, "Prince of Persia", produced by Jerry Bruckheimer and based on a video game, cost more than $150 million to make. "Sex and the City 2", unfortunately, grossed only $52 million. "Iron Man 2," which cost $200 million to make, has already crossed $540 million in worldwide box-office receipts.

Yet, a fabulous picture, like "City Island," with Andy Garcia, an independent movie production, only grossed $4.2 million and lost money.

Variety commented, "Another down weekend as the summer of 2010 continues to struggle to live up to the strength of last year's line-up and box-office performance. All that and a potential log jam of new wide releases coming every weekend through Labor Day."

So, where does this leave us? Should we just stop making movies because we cannot guarantee a theatrical release? Of course not. The indie filmmaker has to look at all forms of digital distribution in order to prove that revenue can be generated to cover the costs of film production and make money for the investor.

Chapter 2
The History of Independent Film

An independent film, or indie film, is a film that is produced outside of a major film studio. Typically, the film is produced by an independent production company and then distributed by a subsidiary of a major studio or independent distributor. It is common that independent films are made with considerably lower budgets than major studio films due to WGA exemptions and the use of lesser known actors and directors.

The roots of independent film can be traced back to the major filmmakers in the 1900s that resisted the control of a trust called the Motion Picture Patents Company or "Edison Trust."

The Motion Picture Patents Company, founded in December 1908, was a trust of all the major film companies (Edison, Biograph, Vitagraph, Essanay, Selig, Lubin, Kalem, American Star, American Pathé), the leading distributor (George Kleine) and the biggest supplier of raw film, Eastman Kodak.

At the time of the formation of the MPPC, Thomas Edison owned most of the major patents relating to motion pictures, including that for raw film. The MPPC vigorously enforced its patents, constantly bringing suits and receiving injunctions against independent filmmakers. Because of this, a number of filmmakers responded by building their own cameras and moving their operations to Hollywood where the distance from Edison's home base of New Jersey made it more difficult for the MPPC to enforce its patents.

The Edison Trust was soon ended by two decisions of the Supreme Court of the United States: one in 1912, which canceled the patent on raw film, and a second in 1915, which cancelled all MPPC patents.

During the Edison era of the early 1900s, many Jewish immigrants had found employment in the US film industry. Under the Edison Trust, they were able to make their mark in a brand-new business: the exhibition of films in storefront theaters called nickelodeons. Within a few years, ambitious men like D. W. Griffith, Samuel Goldwyn, Carl Laemmle, Adolph Zukor, Louis B. Mayer, and the Warner Brothers (Harry, Albert, Samuel, and Jack) had switched to the production side of the business. Soon they were the heads of a new kind of enterprise: the movie studio.

By establishing a new system of production, distribution, and exhibition which was independent of The Edison Trust in New York, these studios opened up new horizons for cinema in the United States. The Hollywood oligopoly replaced the Edison monopoly. Within this new system, a pecking order was soon established which left little room for any newcomers. At the top were the five major studios, MGM, Paramount Pictures, Walt Disney, Warner Bros., and Twentieth Century-Fox. Beneath them were Universal Studios, United Artists, Sony Pictures, Alliance Atlantis and Columbia Pictures. Finally, there was "Poverty Row," a catchall term used to encompass any other smaller studio that managed to fight their way up into the increasingly exclusive movie business.

The studio system quickly became so powerful that some filmmakers once again sought independence as a result. On February 5, 1919 four of the leading figures in American silent cinema (Mary Pickford, Charles Chaplin, Douglas Fairbanks, and D. W. Griffith) formed United Artists, the first independent studio in America. Each held a 20% stake, with the remaining 20% held by lawyer William Gibbs McAdoo.

In 1941, Mary Pickford, Charlie Chaplin, Walt Disney, Orson Welles, Samuel Goldwyn, and David O. Selznick founded the Society of Independent Motion Picture Producers. The Society aimed to preserve the rights of independent producers in an industry overwhelmingly controlled by the studio system. SIMPP fought to end monopolistic practices by the five major Hollywood studios which controlled the production, distribution, and exhibition of films.

In 1942, the SIMPP filed an antitrust suit against Paramount's United Detroit Theatres. The complaint accused Paramount of conspiracy to control first-run and subsequent-run theaters in Detroit. It was the first antitrust suit brought by producers against exhibitors alleging monopoly and restraint of trade.

In 1948, the United States Supreme Court Paramount Decision ordered the Hollywood movie studios to sell their theater chains and to eliminate certain anticompetitive practices. This effectively brought an end to the studio system of Hollywood's Golden Age.

The efforts of the SIMPP and the advent of inexpensive portable cameras during World War II effectively made it possible for any person in America with an interest in making films to write, produce, and direct one without the aide of any major film studio. These circumstances soon resulted in a number of critically acclaimed and highly influential works, including Ruth Orkin and Ray Abrashkin's "Little Fugitive" in 1953, which became the first independent film to be nominated for Academy

Award for Best Original Screenplay at the American Academy Awards.

Unlike the films of the collapsing studio system, these new low-budget films could afford to take risks and explore new artistic territory outside of the classical Hollywood narrative. Based upon a common belief that the official cinema was running out of breath and had become morally corrupt, aesthetically obsolete, thematically superficial, and temperamentally boring, low budget ('B' movies) were very much in demand.

The success of films like "Little Fugitive," which had been made with low (or sometimes non-existent) budgets encouraged a huge boom in popularity for non-studio films.

Like those of the avant-garde, the films of Roger Corman took advantage of the fact that unlike the studio system, independent films had never been bound by its self-imposed production code. Corman's example would help start a boom in independent B-movies in the 1960s, the principle aim of which was to bring in the youth market which the major studios had lost touch with. By promising sex, wanton violence, drug use, and nudity, these films hoped to draw audiences to independent theaters by offering to show them what the major studios could not. Horror and science fiction films experienced a period of tremendous growth during this time.

In 1968, a young filmmaker named George Romero shocked audiences with "Night of the Living Dead," a new kind of intense and unforgiving independent horror film. This film would help set the climate of independent horror for decades to come, such as "The Texas Chain Saw Massacre" in 1974.

Following the advent of television and the Paramount lawsuit, major studios attempted to lure audiences with special effects. Screen gimmicks, Widescreen processes, and technical improvements, such as Cinemascope, stereo sound, 3D and others, were invented in order to retain the dwindling audience by giving them a larger-than-life experience.

By the mid 1960s, the major studios recognized that they did not know how to reach the youth audience. Foreign films, especially European and Japanese cinema, were experiencing a major boom in popularity with young people, who were interested in seeing films with non-traditional subjects and narrative structures. In an attempt to capture this audience, Studios hired a host of young filmmakers (many of whom were mentored by Roger Corman) and allowed them to make their films with relatively little studio control.

In 1967, Warner Bros. offered first-time producer Warren Beatty 40% of the gross on his film "Bonnie & Clyde" instead of a minimal fee. The movie proceeded to gross over $70 million worldwide by 1973.

On May 16, 1969, Dennis Hopper, a young American filmmaker, wrote, directed, and acted in his first film, "Easy Rider." Along with his producer/star/co-writer Peter Fonda, Hopper was responsible for the first completely independent film of New Hollywood. "Easy Rider" debuted at Cannes, received two Oscar nominations, one for best original screenplay and one for

Corman-alum Jack Nicholson's breakthrough performance in the supporting role of George Hanson, an alcoholic lawyer for the ACLU.

Following on the heels of "Easy Rider", United Artists' "Midnight Cowboy," became the first and only X rated film to win the Academy Award for best picture.

Within a month, another young Corman trainee, Francis Ford Coppola, made his debut in Spain at the Donostia-San Sebastian International Film Festival with "The Rain People." Coppola formed a distribution agreement with Warner Bros., allowing him to exploit wide releases for his films without making himself subject to the controlling forces of Hollywood.

These three films provided the major Hollywood studios with both an example to follow and a new crop of talent to draw from. In 1971, Zoetrope (Coppola's company) co-founder George Lucas made his feature film debut with "THX 1138," also released by Zoetrope through their deal with Warner Bros. By the following year, Coppola was offered Paramount's multi-generational gangster epic, "The Godfather." Meanwhile Lucas had obtained studio funding for "American Graffiti" from Universal. In the mid-1970s, the major Hollywood studios continued to tap these new filmmakers for both ideas and personnel, producing idiosyncratic, startling original films such as "Paper Moon," "Dog Day Afternoon" and "Taxi Driver," all of which were met with enormous critical and commercial success.

It can often seem that all members of the New Hollywood generation were independent filmmakers.

Though those mentioned above began with a considerable claim on the title, almost all of the major films commonly associated with the movement were studio projects. The New Hollywood generation soon became firmly entrenched in a revived incarnation of the studio system, which financed the development, production and distribution of their films. Very few of these filmmakers ever independently financed or independently released a film of their own, or ever worked on an independently financed production during the height of the generation's influence.

In retrospect, it can be seen that Steven Spielberg's "Jaws" (1975) and George Lucas's "Star Wars" (1977) marked the beginning of the end for the New Hollywood. With their unprecedented box-office successes, these movies jump-started Hollywood's blockbuster mentality, giving studios a new paradigm as to how to make money in this changing commercial landscape. The focus on high-concept premises, with greater concentration on tie-in merchandise (such as toys), spin-offs into other media (such as soundtracks), and the use of sequels (which had been made more respectable by Coppola's "The Godfather Part II"), all showed the studios how to make money in the new environment.

Like the original independents who fled the Edison Trust to form old Hollywood, the young film school graduates who had fled the studios to explore on-location shooting and dynamic, neo-realist styles and structures ended up replacing the tyrants they had sought to dislodge.

In 1978, Robert Redford, (veteran of New Hollywood and star of "Butch Cassidy and the Sundance Kid") founded the Utah/US Film Festival in an effort to attract more filmmakers to Utah and showcase the potential of independent film. At the time, Redford wanted to present a series of retrospective films, provide filmmaker panel discussions and show new independent films.

In 1991, the festival was officially renamed the Sundance Film Festival, after Redford's famous role as The Sundance Kid. Through this festival, such notable figures as Quentin Tarantino and Steven Soderbergh garnered resounding critical acclaim and unprecedented box-office sales. In 2005, independent studios claimed 15% of the US domestic box office.

The increasing popularity and feasibility of low-budget films have led to a vast increase in the number of aspiring filmmakers — people who have written spec scripts and have hoped to find several million dollars to turn their scripts into successful independent films like "Reservoir Dogs", "Little Miss Sunshine", "Juno" and "Paranormal Activity."

Chapter 3

"The African Queen"

We normally think of independent films as a product of the 1970s and 1980s. Actually, independent films go back as far as the 1950s when studios forced independent thinkers to raise money, make their own films, and use the studios as distributors. One of the most famous independent films became a classic from the moment it hit the big screen, "The African Queen."

"The African Queen," a novel written by English author C.S. Forester, was published in 1935. This unique adventure story about the relationship between a prim spinster and the scruffy boat captain who takes her down the river was kicked around as a potential movie idea for more than 25 years in Hollywood.

The female lead was originally offered to Bette Davis in 1938, with David Niven as Charlie. It was offered to Davis again in 1947, with James Mason, as Charlie, but she had to drop out due to pregnancy. By the time Davis tried out for the role again in 1949, plans were underway for Katharine Hepburn to star.

RKO thought about making it with Charles Laughton and his actress wife Elsa Lanchester, but ultimately the project was scrapped. The thinking was that audiences would not want to see a romance between two middle-aged people. One script reader's notes at RKO reads, "It is dated, incredible, quite outside acceptable dramatic screen material...Its two characters are neither appealing nor sympathetic enough to sustain interest for an entire picture...Both are physically unattractive and their love scenes are distasteful and not a little disgusting. It's no bargain at any price. No amount of rewriting can possibly salvage this dated yarn."

Still, others saw potential in "The African Queen." In 1946, Warner Bros. bought it as a possible vehicle for Bette Davis. That never came to fruition, however, and by 1947, they were trying to unload the property.

Director John Huston, who had always been a fan of the book, wanted desperately to purchase the rights to the property with his producing partner Sam Spiegel as a project for their independent film company, Horizon Pictures. Warner Bros. was willing to sell it to them for $50,000, but even between the two men, they couldn't come up with the cash. They racked their brains to come up with a way to get the money. Finally, Sam Spiegel decided to approach Sound Services, a company that specialized in supplying sound equipment to studios, and see if they would give them the full amount to finance the project. Spiegel promised the company that not only would Horizon pay back every cent, but they would also use Sound Services equipment to make "The African Queen," giving them full credit in the finished film. Sound Services agreed, and the project became theirs.

Huston was adamant that writer James Agee would be the one to help him write the screenplay. Agee was a poet, novelist and film critic whose work Huston had always admired. The two men had become friendly years before when Huston sent Agee a note of appreciation for a review he had written for "The Battle of San Pietro" (1945) in *TIME* magazine, which Huston found "sensitive and perceptive."

When "The African Queen" project came around, Huston thought immediately of his friend Agee and offered him the job. Agee agreed and flew out to California, where he and Huston holed up in a resort hotel outside of Santa Barbara to work on the screenplay. They set a strict regimen for themselves of work and exercise. Though they got a tremendous amount done, Agee did not take care of himself; drinking, smoking, eating too much and not getting enough sleep. Before they could finish the script, Agee had a heart attack and was out of commission for a lengthy recuperation.

Meanwhile, Huston was searching for the ideal leads. Katharine Hepburn was the first one contacted. In 1950, she was touring with the stage production of Shakespeare's "As You Like It," which was currently playing in Los Angeles. Sam Spiegel sent her a copy of the original novel "The African Queen" to read while she was staying at the home of her good friend Irene Selznick. She read it and loved it, knowing that the part of Rose would be perfect for her.

Sam Spiegel came out to visit Hepburn, and the two discussed the project and potential actors to play opposite her. Charlie Allnut was supposed to have a Cockney accent, which limited their choices until Spiegel suggested Humphrey Bogart. They both thought him perfect for the part and simply decided to make his character Canadian, which would solve the problem of the Cockney accent.

John Huston and Humphrey Bogart had worked well together previously on "The Maltese Falcon" (1941), "Across the Pacific" (1942), "The Treasure of the Sierra Madre" (1948), and "Key Largo" (1948).

Neither Huston or Bogart had ever worked with Katharine Hepburn. The actor was somewhat leery of working with her, having heard she could be difficult. However, when Bogie and Huston met with Hepburn, she won them over.

Huston was excited about going on location to Africa and was adamant about shooting it in color, even though it meant more hassles and expense. He felt that color would bring an element of vivid richness to the exotic locale that would bring people into the theater.

Securing financing for the ambitious project was complicated. Most banks were uneasy about putting up money for a film that would be shot in such a remote location. There was unpredictable weather to consider, along with a host of logistical problems. A new London based company called Romulus Productions, however, was eager to lure Hollywood talent overseas, so they took a chance and provided most of the film's financial backing.

Once in Africa, Huston and Spiegel began scouting the dense jungle areas by air. They were looking for a dark, winding body of water like the one described in the original novel. They logged 25,000 flying miles over the areas, and finally, there it was — the Ruiki, a tributary to the Lualaba that was ink black with decaying vegetation. The area in the Congo was so remote that it wasn't marked on most atlases.

Other location problems included sun, rain, snakes, scorpions, crocodiles, tsetse flies, hornets, huge biting black ants, and constant humidity which created mildew everywhere. Further, the African Queen's engine had problems, rope would get tangled in its propellers, and sound from the generator would interfere with shots. One night the Queen sank, and it took three days to raise the boat and get it ready again. There also were no toilets except the outhouse back at camp. The food was OK, but the dishes were washed in infected river water, and virtually everyone in the cast and crew got sick - except for

Bogart and Huston, which they attributed to the fact that they basically lived on imported Scotch. Bogart later said, "All I ate was baked beans, canned asparagus and Scotch whiskey. Whenever a fly bit Huston or me, it dropped dead."

Experts estimate that half of the film was shot in England. For instance, the scenes in which Bogart and Hepburn are seen in the water were all shot in studio tanks at Isleworth Studios, Middlesex, being too dangerous to shoot in Africa.

Sam Spiegel, like Stanley Kramer, represented the generation of independent producers who received their apprenticeships during the tail end of the studio system, and then came into their own as independent producers in the post-Paramount film industry.

Spiegel attracted a top-flight cast with profit participation and salary deferments. Humphrey Bogart received 25 percent of the profits, and Katherine Hepburn took 10 percent. Huston, as director and partner of Horizon received 50 percent of profits. Financing came from Romulus Films which put up production costs in exchange for the exclusive rights to distribution in the eastern hemisphere. In so doing, Spiegel pioneered a production method that has become commonplace for Hollywood independent producers to this day—financing domestic films by pre-selling foreign distribution rights.

Hepburn, Bogart, Huston and Agee went on to earn Oscar nominations, and Bogart won the Best Actor Academy Award for the first and only time in his career.

The roughly $1.3 million gamble turned out to be not only a critical success, earning four Oscar nominations, but a huge commercial hit, pulling in $4.3 million in its first release.

Chapter 4
The Production Code of 1930

From virtually the earliest years of their existence, movies were regarded by many people as a baleful influence on public morality. In the United States, censorship was exercised pretty much by the local community. Many states and individual cities had their own censorship boards that often ordered the deletion of shots, scenes, and/or title cards (during the silent era) before a film could be exhibited within its city limits. Sometimes the films were even banned. The fact that a film was banned somewhere was very often used a marketing ploy to gain publicity in other, less easily offended cities.

However, by 1922 and spurred by several high-profile scandals involving Hollywood celebrities, calls for some type of federal action were heard. In self-defense, motion picture producers passed a succession of moral rules or "codes" meant to guide the content of motion pictures, overseen by former postmaster Will Hays and referred to as the "Hays Code."

Although most producers followed these voluntary rules, after a few years, the guidelines started to relax, and with the advent of sound in the late 1920s, the treatment of crime, violence, sexual infidelity, profanity and even nudity became alarming to a certain section of the population. It is possible that the advent of synchronized sound, with gunshots and swear words now suddenly audible, added to the impact upon the audiences' sensitive ears, and the increasing use of color photography left less and less to the imagination with suggestive costumes and the truthful rendering of bare flesh. So there were more calls for public censorship.

In 1930, a new code (which came to be known as the Hollywood Production Code) was written. The industry accepted it nominally, although many movies stretched it to its limits or simply ignored it, prompting more public outcry. For several years, many filmmakers tried to stretch the code to its limits, if not defy it outright, especially in their use of sexual innuendoes, risqué costumes, and implicitly immoral characters.

In 1934, due partly in response to 1933 films like "Baby Face," "Gold Diggers of 1933," "She Done Him Wrong," "I'm No Angel," and many others, a mechanism was set up to enforce the Code. For the next thirty years, virtually every film produced or exhibited in the United States had to receive a seal of approval from the office of Joseph Breen, the head of the Production Code Administration.

The Production Code Administration did not rate films for different ages. The films were either approved by the Code for release or not, and the major studios would not release a film without the Code's seal of approval. In the 1950s, a few filmmakers and distributors started to actively defy the Code. And, by the 1960s many of the Code's restrictions were loosened if a film's advertising carried a notice recommending it for mature audiences.

The current Ratings System put in place by the Motion Picture Association of America (MPAA) (marked with the letters G, M, R and X) was first established in 1968 (later slightly modified to G, PG, PG-13, R and NC-17). The Ratings System freed filmmakers to include whatever content they desired and submit it to a clandestine board of raters for an official rating. These ratings, however, were not based upon moral values or attitudes (as the Production Code's guidelines had emphasized), but simply upon the content itself and the context in which that subject matter was presented. The MPAA Rating System is marred by somewhat vague quotas for levels of violence, sexual activity or discussions, nudity, and profanity, and these sliding scale quotas were used to divide films into groups with a letter assigned to give viewers an idea of what any given film might or might not contain.

The original Ratings were G for general audiences; M for mature audiences; R for restricted audiences (under 17 required an adult guardian or parent), and X for no children under 17 admitted even with a parent. Very few Hollywood films have actually received an X rating; the most famous being "Midnight Cowboy" and "A Clockwork Orange."

After a number of years, producers again stretched the limits of various ratings, and another public outcry led to the creation of the "PG-13" rating; notably with the release of Steven Spielberg's "Indiana Jones and the Temple of Doom" in 1985.

Below is an excerpt from the original Production Code guidelines followed by Hollywood filmmakers from the mid-1930s until the 1960s.

THE MOTION PICTURE PRODUCTION CODE OF 1930

GENERAL PRINCIPLES

Theatrical motion pictures intended for the theater are primarily to be regarded as Entertainment.

Mankind has always recognized the importance of entertainment and its value in rebuilding the bodies and souls of human beings. But it has always recognized that entertainment can be harmful to the human race. Correct entertainment raises the whole standard of a nation.

Art can be morally good, lifting men to higher levels. This has been done thru good music, great painting, authentic fiction, poetry, drama. In the case of the motion pictures, this effect may be particularly emphasized because no art has so quick and so widespread an appeal to the masses. It has become in an incredibly short period, the art of the multitudes.

Motion pictures need to adhere to its moral obligations. Therefore, no picture should lower the moral standards of those who see it by portraying the following:

- When evil is made to appear attractive and good is made to appear unattractive.
- When the sympathy of the audience is thrown on the side of crime, wrongdoing, evil, sin. The same thing is true of a film that would throw sympathy against goodness, honor, innocence, purity, honesty.
- That in the end the audience feels that evil is good and good is wrong.
- Law, natural or divine, belittled and ridiculed.
- The courts of the land presented as unjust.
- Comedies and farces making fun of good, innocence, morality or justice.

The code further identified situations, which could not be depicted on film, including adultery, husband and wife in the same bed, excess drinking and the like.

Chapter 5
Getting the Public to See Your Movie

Ever since Edison decided to sell the Vitascope Projector, which jump-started the movie industry in 1896, newspapers like the *Buffalo Express* were used to advertise feature attractions such as "Trotting Race at Charter Oak Park" and "The Bathers" to the public.

The past 100 years saw incredible changes in both the film and news industries, leading to changes in how movie theaters tell the public about current showings. Now, instead of printing movie showtimes in the local paper every day, major theaters like AMC, Regal and Carmike have cut back to weekend-only listings or dropped the print versions altogether. In fact, most people now Google names of films or check out movie websites, such as Fandango and Moviefone.

The trend to list movies online is just the latest thorn in the newspaper industry's mortally wounded side. On top of losing the ad revenue from printed movie listings, newspapers find it difficult to compete with free online movie listing sites, which rely on ticket sales and advertising for revenue.

Our local theater, Carmike Cinemas, tried to cut its newspaper advertising budget last year by dropping the movie listings from the daily paper. At first they choose a much smaller listing, which directed users to visit their website for movies and showtimes, including a full listing only on weekends. Eventually, Carmike even purchased a notice in the local paper to explain the change and direct readers to online movie listing websites.

The change was short-lived, as my town's newspaper reading public apparently leans heavily toward the 20-40% of moviegoers who do not get their movie listings online. After residents voiced their complaints, full movie listings returned to the newspaper on a daily basis.

With the prevalence of data-enabled smartphones and continual Internet connections at home, anyone can pull up current showtimes in a manner of seconds.

So, what do the very rich do to get buzz about their films? They attend prestigious film festivals.

The Cannes Film Festival was created in 1959 with a few dozen participants and one projection room built on the canvas roof of the old Palais Croisette. This tiny market gradually emerged as an international event designed, organized and planned to promote cinema. Last year, the Cannes Film Market attracted over 10,000 participants, who took advantage of this unique environment to present and discover almost 4,500 films and projects in more than 30 screening rooms (10 of which are now equipped to show 3D and digital projections).

Let's test your knowledge of Cannes. Who won the Palme d'Or (the highest honor) at the 2009 Cannes Film Festival? Don't know. Most people don't. It was called "The White Ribbon," a black & white drama about World War I. Michael Haneke, an Austrian filmmaker, picked up the Palme d'Or and international critics raved about its "richness." Guess what? The film never found a worldwide distributor because many experts believed that it could not be commercialized for a profit. It found distribution in the United States and played a small run only in the top cities (New York, Los Angeles, Chicago, Dallas-Ft. Worth).

In 2010, the top prize was awarded to a filmmaker from Thailand who had difficulty getting to Cannes due to the burning of buildings by agitators back in Bangkok.

According to official press releases from Cannes 2010, the movie industry continued its downward slide.

Film director Tim Burton and a jury of his cinematic peers (which included Kate Beckinsale and Benicio Del Toro) had a tough task ahead: sorting through a mixed bag of 19 entries competing for top honors at the festival.

Among the handful of films that earned largely favorable reviews were the British ensemble drama "Another Year" from director Mike Leigh and French filmmaker Xavier Beauvois' "Of Gods and Men," a tale of martyrdom based on the true story of seven monks beheaded during Algeria's civil war in 1996.

Two other past Palme d'Or winning directors also had films in the running — Britain's Ken Loach ("The Wind that Shakes the Barley") with his Iraq War thriller "Route Irish" and Iran's Abbas Kiarostami ("Taste of Cherry") with his cryptic love story "Certified Copy," starring Juliette Binoche.

Mexican director Alejandro Gonzalez Inarritu, whose "Babel" won him the Cannes directing prize in 2006, competed again with the well-received "Biutiful," featuring a stellar performance from Javier Bardem as a father supporting his family through various criminal rackets in Barcelona.

South Korea's Lee Chang-dong also earned warm reviews for "Poetry," his gentle drama about a grandmother who finds solace writing poems amid the onset of Alzheimer's disease and has troubles with her brooding grandson.

The lone American film in competition — Doug Liman's "Fair Game," starring Naomi Watts as ousted CIA operative Valerie Plame, and Sean Penn as her husband, Joe Wilson — received solid, but restrained praise.

In 2010, big name directors mostly screened their films outside the competition spotlight. Among them were Ridley Scott with the opening-night premiere of "Robin

Hood," Oliver Stone with "Wall Street: Money Never Sleeps," Woody Allen with "You Will Meet a Tall Dark Stranger," and Stephen Frears with "Tamara Drewe," a light, breezy tale that Cannes crowds cheered amid the generally gloomy tone of the awards contenders.

According to the inside-finance crowd at Cannes, the pre-sale market (in which a film project is valued and pre-sold to various international territories based upon the elements involved prior to shooting) has dried up and may never come back. That, combined with fewer banks lending to producers, means equity investment is more important than ever. Even those private lenders still left in the game said they want to fully finance their own movies with equity.

The trend at this year's market was for sales agents to make one or two key pre-sales, encouraging financiers to get in at that point. However, distributors were standing pat with folded arms, waiting for high-quality, completed product. In years past, buyers used to jump in throughout a movie's production, locking distribution rights for themselves. No more.

There wasn't much interest in finished projects either. Normally, there are three or four completed films that get buyers salivating. Sony Pictures Classics was the only studio to flash its cash, buying domestic rights to three titles: "Another Year," "Of Gods and Men" and "In a Better World." Relativity Media bought the US sci-fi movie "Skyline." And IFC acquired the US rights to Xavier Dolan's *Un Certain Regard* entry "Heartbeats."

And, of course, troubled starlet Lindsay Lohan made an appearance. She rolled the dice in her DUI probation case in a big way -- because TMZ reported that she headed off to Cannes skipping her alcohol rehab class. TMZ reported that the judge ordered Lohan to show proof the following week that she had completed 13 alcohol rehab educations classes, but she only completed nine. Eventually, Lindsay was held in contempt and served 13 days in prison. The press release said that she was released on "good behavior" and that the "prison was overcrowded."

As far as the negative mood in Cannes was concerned, many blamed it on the freak 30-foot wave that drenched this harbor city on opening day. Some blamed the volcano in Iceland, which delayed the flights of several festival-goers, resulting in a more jet-lagged and grouchy audience than usual. Others blamed the economic jitters that have swept the European Union and the rest of the world. Perhaps all of those current events accounted for the relatively subdued mood of the festival, which used to be known for buxom starlets and outrageous publicity antics.

Chapter 6

Learn to Become a Producer

In the early-20th century, the producer controlled the film project. With the demise of Hollywood's studio system in the 1950s, creative control began to shift to the director.

Changes in movie distribution and marketing in the 1970s and 1980s gave rise to the modern-day phenomenon of the Hollywood blockbuster, which tended to bring power back into the hands of the producer. While marketing and advertising for films accentuates the role of the director, it is usually the producer who has the greatest control.

Traditionally, the producer is considered the chief of staff, while the director is in charge of the line. This "staff and line" organization mirrors that of most large corporations and the military. Under this arrangement, the producer has overall control of the project and can terminate the director, but the director actually makes the film happen.

Many people claim to be producers, and the title is thrown around with seemingly little understanding of the duties and responsibilities, so in order to be clear, let's first review producer titles and responsibilities.

Producer: The producer initiates, coordinates, supervises and controls all aspects of the motion picture production process, including creative, financial, technological and administrative operations. The producer is involved throughout all phases of production from inception to completion, including coordination, supervision and control of all other talents and crafts, subject to the provisions of their collective bargaining agreements and personal service contracts.

Executive Producer: The executive producer raises the money and oversees the financial, administrative, and creative aspects of production. He usually coordinates all producer activities and controls the checking account.

Associate Producer: She represents the producer, who may need to share financial, creative, or administrative tasks. Often, the associate producer title is granted as a courtesy to someone instrumental in the inception of the project or to someone who made a major financial or creative contribution to the production.

Line Producer: He is the most important cost control person in the field. He oversees a film's budget and day-to-day activities. He supervises the physical aspects of the making of a motion picture and is rarely involved in the creative decision-making process.

Administrative Producer: The administrative producer reports to the Board of Directors of the film studio. Freelancers are employed by the administrative producer for specific tasks, such as press and publicity activities, design, production, and management.

For decades, movie producers had one of the cushiest gigs in Hollywood. Studios kept stables of them around — all expenses paid — to shepherd movies through their various stages: inception, the nitty-gritty of filming, post-production, and publicity.

The job was appealing for its variety, as the major studios sought films ranging from teenage blockbusters to arty dramas to dark comedies. Producers also commanded respect because, as powerful middlemen, they could interface with studio management at the major studios.

Fortunately, the production process has gone through a lot of changes, and those who no longer bring value to the table are long gone.

Studios, reeling from declines in DVD sales, have sharply reduced the number of producers kept on retainer. For example, Warner Bros. has slashed producer deals by 20 percent since 2008, and more reductions are on the way as current deals expire. This has left a generation of producers having to find a new way to pay their development bills.

At the same time, the number of movies being made has shrunk drastically. Half the independent distributors have folded over the last couple of years, and the major studios have cut back. Paramount Pictures will only release 15 films this year.

Hawk Koch, whose producing credits include the 2000 thriller "Frequency," notes that there are still producer success stories, like "Paranormal Activity." The inexpensive horror flick has generated about $193 million in global box-office revenue and has a sequel on the way.

Other success stories include Basil Iwanyk, who remade "Clash of the Titans," and Judy Cairo & Michael A. Simpson, who brought us "Crazy Heart," starring Jeff Bridges.

According to IMDb, some of the biggest movie winners in various categories include:

Worldwide Revenue	"Titanic"	$1,845,034,000
G-Rating	"Finding Nemo"	$339,714,978
Movies That Never Hit #1	"My Big Fat Greek Wedding"	$241,438,208
Romantic Comedy	"Hitch"	$43,142,214
Fastest Studio to $1 Billion	Paramount	189 Days

Let's face it. Everyone wants to make the next "The Blair Witch Project." Produced by Haxen Films in 1999 for $60,000 (production plus marketing), the movie earned $140M domestically and $108M in foreign sales.

Do you remember any of the names associated with the film? Did they ever make another film?

According to trivia websites, the three principal actors, Heather Donahue, Joshua Leonard and Michael Williams shot nearly all of the completed film. The actors were requested to interview the townspeople, who often, unbeknownst to the actors, were planted by the director. As a result, the expressions on the actors' faces were unrehearsed and compellingly legitimate.

The actors were given no more than a 35-page outline of the mythology behind the plot before shooting began. All lines were improvised and nearly all the events in the film were unknown to the three actors beforehand and were often on-camera surprises to them all.

Some theatergoers experienced nausea from the handheld camera movements and actually had to leave to vomit. In some Toronto theaters, ushers asked patrons who were prone to motion sickness to sit in aisle seats in case they needed to exit quickly.

One of the video cameras used by the actors was bought at Circuit City. After filming was completed, the producers returned the camera for a refund, making their budget money go even further.

This film is in the *Guinness Book of World Records* for "Top Budget to Box Office Ratio" for a mainstream feature film. "The Blair Witch Project" took a mere 8 days to shoot.

The movie held the record for the highest-grossing independent movie of all time until October 2002, when it was surpassed by "My Big Fat Greek Wedding".

As we know, not all movies can be breakouts like "The Blair Witch Project" and "My Big Fat Greek Wedding." Of course, this does not stop the independent moviemaker from reaching for the brass ring.

Let's look at some of the gross numbers reported by the major studios (reported in millions):

Paramount	$1,431
Sony/Columbia	$1,188
Warner Bros	$1,153
Buena Vista	$1,147
Universal	$1,047
20th Century Fox	$815
New Line Cinema	$426
Lionsgate	$367
MGM/UA	$322
Fox Searchlight	$102
Miramax	$98
Rogue Pictures	$73

If you add up the totals for the top 12 major houses, you come up with approximately $8.6 billion in gross revenue. A detailed analysis indicates that the industry has become more and more reliant on foreign sales, DVD and other distribution channels, including soundtrack releases, to make money.

Unfortunately, this is a bad sign.

The dollar value of foreign rights of films made by US filmmakers has dropped precipitously while homegrown films are more desired by local audiences. With a slew of foreign countries now developing their second-generation wealth, young adults in those foreign countries prefer to see pictures about their local culture, not what the US exports. On top of that, DVD sales keep declining as Netflix and Blockbuster continue to cut costs to fight Internet sales. Recently, Blockbuster announced that they would close 960 stores and develop kiosks to fight Red Box, the $1 DVD rental program usually found outside your local 7-11 or supermarket.

So, is it important to get into a major studio for distribution? Not really. Many movies are made and distributed through independent distributors. According to IMDb there are 113 movie distribution companies with global connections.

The six major movie studios compete against smaller movie production and distribution companies including Sony Classics and Lionsgate. However, they are buying fewer and fewer films since they have had difficulty raising money in the public markets.

From 1998 through 2005, independent DreamWorks SKG ranked 7th in sales. In February 2006, DreamWorks was acquired by Viacom, Paramount's parent company. However, Steven Spielberg (one of the founders and an active participant) recently took control of the company with an infusion of financing from India.

Today, major studios are primarily backers and distributors of films whose actual production is largely handled by independent companies—either long-running entities or ones created for and dedicated to the making of a specific film. Since they've been reduced to nothing more than advertising outfits, why does all the power and prestige still reside within the studio gates?

Marketing determines the success or failure of a film. Opening weekend means everything, and high-octane marketing campaigns – costing upwards of $40 million – can make a mediocre film number one in box-office revenue.

In the past, specialty divisions often simply acquired distribution rights to pictures with which the studio had no prior involvement. Now, major studios are copying that proven formula and getting out of production, instead focusing on market research, script concept, cofinancing, sales forecasting, distribution, marketing and cross merchandising.

This metamorphosis provides a savvy independent producer a great opportunity to deliver quality finished product to a distributor who can get it into theaters.

Chapter 7
Prepare to Meet Your Investor

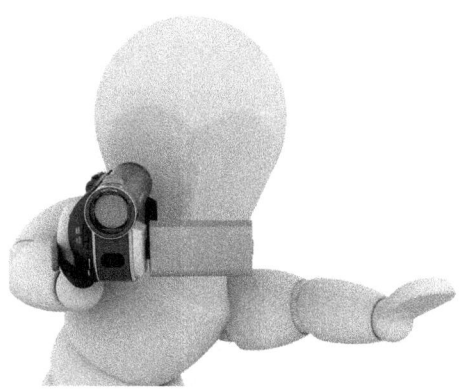

Head out to the real world and ask for money. And, when they turn you down, take it in stride and go out again. Eventually, you will succeed. Most people fail because they do not sufficiently prepare to endure the tough questions that investors throw at wannabe producers. Sophisticated investors will judge you quickly and ask tough questions on a wide variety of subjects. Investors, including myself, love to test your ability to survive tough battles with actors, writers, crew and all of the people needed to make your film a reality.

So, when you ask me for $5.5 million to make a film, I am surely going to ask you, "So, have you made a $5.5 million picture before? Tell me what you did right and wrong." If you have not made a multimillion dollar picture before and you are asking me to take all the risk of financing your "pet" project… well, it is not going to happen.

There are books you can read. There are courses you can take. You can never prepare too much for your meetings. However, textbook knowledge and classroom time is no substitute for real-world experience.

Here are my thoughts on key subjects, which I have excerpted from my book, *Going from W2 to 1099*. Where possible, I reworded some text to address the specific issues that filmmakers face.

Advertising

Advertising is a form of communication that persuades potential customers to attend your movie. Experts will tell you that you must advertise to win the opportunity to sell seats. Although that may be true for most corporations, I am afraid to say that if you follow most of their advice you will pay out a lot and see very little in return. That is because independent filmmakers must think differently than the big corporations.

I believe that you are the advertisement. Potential investors will buy from you and customers will see your film, if they have a need and can justify the price. As a result, I have found that most print advertising, Internet advertising, radio and TV spots do not work unless you plan to spend tens of thousands of dollars in creating your "brand." Otherwise, you should spend your limited resources on working your personal "networks" to your advantage.

Advisors

Surround yourself with lots of "unpaid" advisors. You never know when an emergency will arise and you will need to talk to someone who has a vested interest in your success. Advisors can come from family, social circles and networking groups. If possible, ask more than one person the same question. You will be surprised how many people can shed different viewpoints on different situations.

Beating the Odds

When I was younger, I always felt that I could beat the odds. I figured that someone had to be able to do it; so, why not me? After many years of experimentation (and many eye-opening and heart-wrenching rounds of "trial and error"), I finally concluded that no one can beat the odds. One may have a favorable position for a long period of time, but unfortunately, most of the good luck runs out and they, too, find themselves in the unenviable position of rebuilding their success.

So, look at all situations, calculate your odds of success and make your decision. Going with your gut feeling succeeds only in the movies and has very little chance of survival in the marketplace.

Branding

It's all about branding, no matter how small you are. People won't remember what you do, unless they remember something about you. Use visual reminders whenever possible, and make sure your message is consistent. If you don't solidify your message, your potential investor will not give you a chance to succeed.

Develop a logo to identify your company and use it on all of your marketing material, including your business card and website(s).

Business Cards

I love business cards. At one point, I had six different cards to represent the six different products/services I was promoting. It got a little bit ridiculous at networking events, when I pulled out six different cards looking for the right one to give to a potential client. Eventually, I put all of my products/services into a single web portal and created a single business card.

Business cards are inexpensive; so do not go cheap at this crucial step. Use color and have a designer develop a logo for you. Brand image is crucial. Pick your company's name and your title carefully since they have to resonate with potential customers. Make sure you put your e-mail, telephone number, and website info on the card.

Business Plans

A good business plan sells you and your product. It must describe a problem and your proposed solution. Always put your words into writing. It gives you an advantage over the competition that thinks they can sell with verbal promises.

Business Writing

Take a business-writing course. There are plenty at the local community college. The last time you learned how to write was in 4th grade. Learn to use the grammar checker built into your word processor and learn how to use the English language for maximum effect – expertly crafted, persuasive words help paint your solution. You do not have to impress people with big words, in fact big words work against you. Simple sells; simple, but expertly crafted.

Competitors

I once met a businessperson who claimed he had no competitors. His arrogance immediately turned me off and I told him that I could not do business with him. God must have been listening, because he was out of business within a year. Everyone has competitors, some in the most unlikely places. Regardless of your competitor, you must always be able to show the competitive advantage of your project. Otherwise, there is no compelling argument for a potential investor to part with his hard-earned cash.

Con Artists

No matter how old or wise you get, you will still get conned. And you never see them coming. The best ones are very smooth and polished. Sadly, when I am conned, I don't know about it until after the fact. It never gets easier, and it still hurts, regardless of your level of wealth.

Debt

You need to keep your debt down as low as possible because interest payments can kill you. However, I prefer debt to giving away equity because if a project is successful, an increased equity position will put more money in my pocket. Start with a few credit cards in your company's name, and then go for a line of credit. You may have to give a personal guarantee and put up collateral, but you will ultimately be able to borrow against the business and keep your personal assets safe.

Direct Mail

There are only two ways to get customers: meet them in person (Press the Flesh) or use third party advertising to get them to call you. I have found that Direct Mail and its related products (e.g., door hangers, Robo Calls, PPC, postcards, brochures, catalogs and the like) cost a lot of money and do not work. Spend your money to meet people. Let them get to know you.

Economy

Currently, we are in a terrible economy marked by high persistent unemployment, tight credit, loss of jobs, declining real estate values, and a wholesale assault on our free markets. Do not be surprised if wealthy investors cannot help you now. That does not mean that they may not want to invest somewhere down the road. Keep in touch.

False Optimism

As an independent filmmaker, you need to stay positive, search for new ideas and find money. This doesn't mean that you should believe or spout false optimism to yourself and your closest colleagues. Deal with reality. If you don't, you'll lose credibility and you can never win it back.

First Impression

It takes just 2-3 seconds for someone to evaluate you when they meet you for the first time. In an instant, the other person forms an opinion about you based on your appearance, your body language, demeanor, mannerisms, and how you are dressed. Don't waste the opportunity.

With every new encounter, you are carefully evaluated. You can never reverse or erase first impressions. So, make those first encounters count. Treat everyone with respect. However, judge them as they judge you. Do not waste your time with someone that cannot help you.

Focus

Once you have laid the foundation with your plan, strategies, and goals, stay focused on getting to your destination one step at a time. It's very easy to become distracted and let everyone else's goals, plans, wants and needs interrupt yours.

Funding

Funding is gasoline. Without it, your project goes nowhere. Make sure you always have funding. Make sure you get it before you need it, even if you have to pay an annual fee and keep it in reserve. I've seen many projects run out of steam because they could not find financing during the tough times.

I never thought about interest rates as long as I could put the money into projects that yielded more than my carrying costs. This is an important factor to consider. Staying active and solvent provide the means to succeed.

Generating Ideas

When you run out of ideas, pick up any object and write down everything that comes to mind about it. For example, pick up a box of cereal and jot down everything you can think about it, such as the color, shape, size, weight and taste. Then, compare it to similar things, such as those that have the same color and shape. Think about the box of cereal in terms of how things are categorized as small, medium, and large. You'll be amazed by how many ideas you can generate from a single object.

Don't restrain your ideas. Some of my best ideas came from seemingly illogical thought. I know I have a winner when I tell my wife, and she replies, "Normal people don't do it that way."

Creativity is an asset which must be cultivated.

Getting In Line

As a kid, we always tried to "cut" in line by walking to the front to join our friends. I was small, but smart, so I had big friends who wanted me to befriend me. Even when people yelled at us, they backed off quickly when my bigger friends showed them a clenched fist.

As adults, you don't have those privileges. If you want to be successful, get in line, and wait your turn just like the rest of us. There are no shortcuts to the front of the line.

Ideas

Keep a pencil and pad of paper with you at all times. When an idea pops into your head, write it down, and put it in an idea drawer or folder. Don't judge your ideas. Let your advisors and the marketplace do that. Periodically, pull out all of your notes from your idea drawer. If the idea is bad, throw it away. If it is good, work on it.

Ingenuity

Your mind is the very source of creative expression. The choice is always there. Never let anyone tell you that you're crazy or that your idea(s) won't work. Even if you are crazy, who cares? One tweak of your "crazy" could turn it into the latest smash hit. Success comes from persistence, and all good ideas eventually rise to the top. An idea just needs time, money and effort.

Minor Successes

Enjoy the minor successes of your day. It will make you and everyone around you feel better. Successes, even the little ones, are a state of mind. Success isn't defined by others or your bank account. Look for the little successes when you wake up and just before you go to bed.

Motivation

Motivation has its roots in the Great Depression. There are many stories of young teens having to work to help their parents pay the mortgage and put food on the table. With a severe shortage of jobs, they sold newspapers and ice cream in the neighborhood. When they had enough cash, they bought goods and sold them from pushcarts.

Remember that people are motivated by lots of things, not just money. The right title, job responsibilities or terms of employment, such as flexible hours, can be just as attractive as money. Try to understand the needs of your people in order to create an environment of success.

Perseverance

Perseverance is the only way to become successful. Pursuing potential customers over and over again in order to complete sales is a constant of selling, which never fluctuates.

Pitch Festivals

After you write a movie script, go to a pitch festival and "pitch" it. You may not sell your script, but you'll have the time of your life trying to convince a total stranger that he should give you Tom Cruise's or Robert Downey, Jr.'s private phone number and $30 million to make your movie.

Planning

If you don't know where you're going, any path will take you there. It's better to take the time to write down a plan of action. If your plan of action doesn't work, change the plan. Don't go naked into the night because you'll surely spend a lot of time and energy shooting blanks.

Press Releases

Press releases are a low-cost, effective way to get publicity. Major search engines scan for press releases all the time. Learn to write and publish your own press releases. You'll save a lot of money, because no one knows you better than you do.

Relevance

I get many phone calls from telemarketers and salespeople. I try to listen to all of them because I never know when I'll hear something that might help me with my business. If it isn't relevant, I don't want to waste my time or theirs.

Companies that succeed in the market strengthen customer relevance by methodically and systematically understanding the customer's need. They then demonstrate total commitment by creating an offering that meets every aspect of that need.

When I pitch a product or service, I use the same principle in order to connect with potential customers and clients.

Risk Taking

You must be willing to take a risk. This is a common theme among successful people. They see an opportunity and the high-degree of risk that comes with it, but they go ahead and approach the opportunity anyway. Lose the fear of failure. Get rid of it. It's holding you back. We learn the most valuable lessons in life from failure, not success. The most successful people will tell you that they failed many times before succeeding.

Setting Priorities (A-B-C)

It's easy in the rush of life to respond to everything that comes up at the moment it happens. Your overreaction is a recipe for madness and disaster. You will lose control and jeopardize your project. You cannot afford to react emotionally when the rest of the world is not thinking appropriately.

When we don't set priorities, we follow the path of least resistance. We'll pick and sort through the things we need to do and work on the easiest ones—leaving the more difficult and less fun tasks for a "later" time, which often never comes. Or, worse, it comes just before the action needs to be finished, throwing us into a whirlwind of activity, stress, and regret. Creating a strategy to prioritize your day, your week, and your month needs to be natural. Success comes through concerted effort on a variety of factors.

My top priorities are always revenue. Without revenue, all of my other priorities become meaningless.

Socializing

Successful moviemakers love to socialize and meet people. When I started my first business in 1984, I thought that success would come from developing a great product. Sadly, I didn't know that people would not only judge the product, but they would also judge me.

Learn to get over awkward moments and go up to strangers and tell them about your project. It's very difficult at first. However, if you don't learn to socialize, you'll be better off working for someone else behind the scenes. As a filmmaker, you're always on stage. Mastering the ability to smartly, effortlessly, and effectively "work the room" is a critical skill.

Success

Many people define success by money, power, and title. I define success by a feeling in my heart. If you feel successful, then you probably are. Look for the little successes along the way, and remind yourself that life is good.

Trend Spotting

Trend spotting is truly the key to making a great film. Successful moviemakers understand current events and look for future trends. If you keep up with what's going on socially, environmentally, and with business and consumers, you will definitely create a great idea.

Be creative in your thinking. Anticipate what moviegoers will want to see—not only right now, but also years down the road. Essentially, anything that has staying power is a trend. It has social, political, and economic significance. Trends develop gradually and follow a sequence of events. Fads, meanwhile, come and go in a flash.

Read newspapers and magazines, especially from the East and West coasts, where trends are often born. Go online and read blogs. Watch TV. Talk to teenagers. Look at companies like Wal-Mart to see where their profits come from. Basically, do anything you can to stay on top of what's hot and what's not—and what will be hot in the future. Pop culture is constantly changing and you want to have your hand on its pulse to be a successful and viable filmmaker.

The beauty is that it is within your power as a filmmaker to act on the trends that you spot. You're in control of your own destiny. So, when you see a trend coming, plan for it and jump in when the timing is right. Independent moviemakers can actually outflank major studios, because they are too big to move quickly. The nimble indie producer can make success happen by just being able to understand the zeitgeist and make actionable decisions that are ahead of the curve.

Viral Marketing

Viral marketing uses preexisting social networks to increase brand awareness and to achieve other marketing objectives (such as DVD sales) through self-replicating viral processes.

The viral marketing message can be delivered by word-of-mouth or enhanced by the networking effects of the Internet. Viral promotions may take the form of video clips, interactive Flash games, advergames, e-books, brandable software, images and text messages.

In conclusion, prepare for every encounter and do not expect investors to jump up and down with joy at your screenplay. We see too many and get jaded with all of the poorly written material that we see on a daily basis.

For more ideas on how to pitch your film, please visit

http://showbizmanagementadvisors.com or

http://booksbyjeffreytaylor.com

Chapter 8

Managing Investor Attitudes

Let me share with you a recent conversation I had with a cold call from an independent moviemaker who found me on the Internet.

Me: (answer phone) Jeffrey Taylor.

Filmmaker: *Jeffrey Taylor, please.*

Me: This is Jeffrey Taylor.

Filmmaker: *I saw your website and it said that I could call you to pitch my movie idea.*

Me: Yes.

Filmmaker: *Can I tell you about my movie?*

Me: Did you read the section that tells you how to pitch me?

Filmmaker: *Yes.*

Me: That's great. But, remember I do not want to hear your logline, synopsis, treatment or anything about the script. I want you to focus on the economics of your film, why you think people will get up off the couch and pay $6.50 to go to the movies.

Filmmaker: *Perhaps, we can talk at another time?*

Me: O.K. Please read my articles on pitching. Do your homework and talk economics. Remember, this is show business. We both need to make money.

*****

When the movie industry needed cash in the 1980s, it tapped individual investors through brokerage firms. That strategy ran its course, and in the 1990s, German tax credits became the next sales pitch; funnel money to movies via a legislative loophole and take immediate tax deductions.

As recently as last year, Goldman Sachs, JP Morgan Chase, and many of the giant hedge funds poured billions of dollars into groups of movies called "slates." Wall Street believed that investors could maximize returns and minimum risk if they invested in six or more movies at once.

Unfortunately, one cannot predict success and slates can also fail. As a result, the big studios ran out of money. Their upfront needs were too big — Universal's last round of private financing, which closed last September, totaled about $3 billion.

As of June 2009, Steven Spielberg, who amid the credit crunch had been having a tough time raising money to finance the re-acquisition of his DreamWorks studio, received billions of dollars from a well-financed company in India.

The filmmaker's lead bank, JPMorgan Chase, had received a commitment for about $150 million -- nearly half of the $325-million loan that Spielberg hoped to have in place. Only then did Spielberg's financial partner, India's Reliance Entertainment, begin forking over its matching equity portion so the director could start making movies. Later in the year, Spielberg and Reliance paid Paramount Pictures about $27 million to buy 17 projects that DreamWorks had been developing at their former studio home.

In 2010, the credit crunch has put the brakes on outside film financing. Hollywood executives fear the glut created by the recent spate of overproduction will be felt for years. Competition is especially brutal in the market for small movies. Oscar-aspiring independent films were once seen as the most attractive segment of the industry. That's because sizable profits could be made on films that required relatively little investment. That calculation prompted the major Hollywood studios to launch divisions aimed at exploiting that market niche. However, the flood of indie films drove up marketing costs, as each film spent more to compete in the crowded advertising landscape.

Now that the economic crisis has washed away much of that money, a wannabe moviemaker needs to find financing in "less traditional" areas and give up more of their potential profits to convince investors to take on the "risk of failure."

The most sought-after investors are called "accredited investors." Under the Securities Act of 1933, a company that offers or sells its securities must register the securities with the SEC or find an exemption from the registration requirements. The Act provides companies with a number of exemptions. For some of the exemptions, such as rules 505 and 506 of Regulation D, a company may sell its securities to what are known as "accredited investors."

I invest in indie films and encourage people to tell me about their projects. As a result, I get anywhere from 2-3 emails a day pitching me a movie project. In general, most of them fail to get me motivated to look at the attachments, which typically include a business plan, movie script, trailers and hyperlinks to their project websites.

Most people assume that I am already in the supermarket and ready to buy. What moviemakers fail to understand is that you must first get me to want to go to your supermarket.

So, here are some ideas, which will get my attention in your email:

Tell me why movies are a good investment and how they are better than alternative investments such as gold, oil, platinum, diamonds and real estate.

Tell me why your movie is better than other movies without going into how great or unique your is story. Tell me why the market needs your movie.

Tell me why I should invest in your project. What's in it for me?

Tell me what you have done to move your project forward. Are you on first base, second base, etc. in your journey to get your project done?

Tell me who is associated with your project. Tell me who you know. Tell me who has already put in money. Don't tell me about tax incentives, product placement or deferred equity from distributors. That is not real money. They are the promise of money. And, if you want me to be the first investor, tell me why others have already turned you down.

Tell me which distributors you have talked to. Many of them will tell you the market value of your project. This way I know what the maximum amount your picture can cost and still make a profit.

In general, movie investors are arrogant and condescending. We set very high standards and when we look to recover our investment, we like to see it double within three years.

If you cannot accomplish that with a documented strategy, I will not listen to you.

Sophisticated investors invest in people who are in it for the long haul and have the ability to withstand the pain of others trying to knock them down. This is not a part-time job. Amateurs need not apply.

Trust me on this one. If you can get my attention in a cold call email, I will probably download your files, look at your websites, read your attachments and carry on an intelligent conversation with you. Otherwise, you are wasting both my time and yours.

Chapter 9

Basic Accounting Terms

Before we discuss budgeting later in the book, let's make sure you have a good understanding of basic accounting terms and phrases.

DEBITS AND CREDITS

These are the backbone of any accounting system. Every accounting entry in a general ledger contains both a debit and a credit, and all debits must equal all credits. If they don't, the general ledger will be out of balance.

Therefore, your accounting system, whether it is a spreadsheet or automated accounting software, must have a mechanism to ensure that all the entries balance. Depending on what type of account you are dealing with, a debit or credit will either increase or decrease the account balance.

DEBITS AND CREDITS VS. ACCOUNT

Account	Debit	Credit
Assets	Increases	Decreases
Liabilities	Decreases	Increases
Equity	Decreases	Increases
Income	Decreases	Increases
Expenses	Increases	Decreases

Notice that for every increase in one account, there is an opposite (and equal) decrease in another. That's what keeps the individual and overall account in balance. Also notice that debits always go on the left and credits on the right.

For example, let's say an investor gives you $10,000 for your movie. Your accounting entry would be:

| Cash | $10,000 | |
| Investor Equity | | $10,000 |

Let's look at another example. Let's say you need to buy some computer paper for your printer.

Supplies	$ 100		
Cash		$	100

That's it. Accounting doesn't really get much harder. Everything else is just a variation on the same theme.

Assets and Liabilities

Balance sheet accounts include assets, liabilities and equity. When you set up your chart of accounts, there will be separate sections and numbering schemes for the assets, liabilities and equities that make up the balance sheet.

Simply stated, assets are items of value that your movie production owns. The cash in your bank account is an asset. So is the company car that you drive. Assets are the objects, rights and claims owned by and having value for the company.

Since your company has a right to the future collection of money from distributors, theaters and movie studios, you will become very familiar with accounts receivable. The computer equipment in your studio is an asset. If your firm owns real estate or other tangible property, those are considered assets as well.

There may also be intangible assets owned by your company. Patents, the exclusive right to use a trademark and goodwill from the acquisition of another company are considered intangible assets.

Think of liabilities as the opposite of assets. These are the obligations of one company to another. Accounts payable are liabilities, since they represent your company's obligation to pay a vendor, supplier or tradesperson. So is the loan you took out from your bank.

After the liability section in both the chart of accounts and the balance sheet comes owners' equity. This is the difference between assets and liabilities.

Think of the balance sheet as today's snapshot of the assets and liabilities your company has acquired since the first day of business. The income statement, in contrast, is a summation of the income and expenses from the first day of the accounting period, which could be a month, a quarter or a year.

Revenues and Expenses

Further down in the chart of accounts comes the income and expense accounts. Most investors want to see where a production company derived income and how it was spent. Most production companies have only a few income accounts, but some have dozens, if not hundreds, of expense accounts. Tracking expenses enable you to monitor variances against budget and help prepare documents for the IRS or unions.

On the revenue side, you need to focus on cash flows you will receive from those whom you selling your rights. Most first-timers go to a film festival and try to get a film distribution company to buy the distribution rights (domestic, foreign or both) to their movie. If you are successful, you will probably get back $3 dollars for every $1 dollar you or your investors put into your movie. Of course, a lot of that revenue must cover your production, deferred compensation and marketing expenses.

The more successful you become, the more likely you will be able to sell your product to distributors higher up in the food chain. If you are like others, you will probably sell your first movie to a direct-to-DVD distributor or sell it yourself on the Internet, the second one to a local/regional distributor, your third one to a national distributor and your fourth one to a global/international distributor.

Remember: hitting many singles appeals to investors, not the occasional home run. Steady, consistent returns indicate that you know your industry, have achieved a proven track record, and have the highest probability of hitting a home run on your proposed project. Investors love winners, not wannabes.

Chapter 10

Preparing Budgets

More than 4,000 movies are produced worldwide each year. In the United States alone, around $9 billion is spent on theatrical tickets. While many of the movies are co-financed and produced by major Hollywood studios, independent investors, including private investors, equity firms and hedge funds, have changed the way films are produced.

Skyrocketing production and marketing costs in Hollywood coupled with a decline in attendance of the movie-going public have made the standard studio business model a difficult proposition. In the wake of that, smaller production companies have risen up by creating entertainment for a fraction of the cost of the major studios. Many of these films will be released theatrically; others will be sold direct-to-video. Some will win awards at film festivals. Sadly, many will never be seen.

Many independent films have budgets as low as $50,000, while others rival those of major studio films. A typical film targeted for direct-to-video release can run in the range of $300,000 - $500,000; theatrical releases start at $1-2 million dollars.

How well these films do financially depends on how they are distributed. Most feature-length motion pictures find a distributor that will at least distribute a direct-to-video release of the picture. This deal can take many forms. The distributor may offer a small sum up front (an "advance") with a split of the distributor's profits, or the distributor may offer a large lump sum to cover the film's budget, and then offer a split of the profits. Or, the distributor may offer a deal that only includes profit sharing with no money paid upfront. In most cases, profit sharing arrangements usually provide the production company 40% of the box office less distribution and marketing expenses. As always, the more successes you have under your belt, the more leverage you have at the negotiating table.

Distributor's profits come from the viewing public. A film that has a theatrical release generally has a 50-50 split of the box-office receipts. Video sales carry a similar split. So, a film with a $2 million budget will need to gross $8 million to break even. Obviously, smaller budgets will not need to earn as much to cover expenses, pay back investors, and provide generous returns to the moviemaker.

A typical budget is broken down by line items. Each line item represents a different type of expense that the production plans to pay. Traditionally, feature film budgets are divided into two sections, above-the-line and below-the-line. Above-the-line items include writer's salaries, story rights, producer's fees, director's fees, and talent salaries.

The below-the-line section of the budget is usually broken down into production, post-production and distribution. Production items include the production staff, extras, the art department (set design, set construction, set dressing, and props), wardrobe, make-up and hair, the camera department (electrical, lighting and camera), sound, special effects, location expenses, transportation, overtime and film/tape stock.

The post-production portion includes the editorial department, the sound department, the visual effects department, music rights, music composition and scoring, film laboratory costs, post-production facility costs, sound facility costs, film and videotape/audio stock.

The distribution section includes publicity, film prints, video tape duplication, and other costs for distributing the film.

In 1975, I graduated with an MBA in Finance from the University of Chicago and immediately went to work for Citibank in New York City. In my first year, I came in at 20% under budget for my department. I was extremely proud of myself. At the end of the year, they cut my next year's budget by 20% due to my efficiencies in bringing projects in under budget. I learned early in my career to never again bring anything in under budget.

In the movie industry, we have to budget or we cannot raise funds from investors. Now, here is the problem.

If you have never budgeted a picture before, how to do you know what to budget for? And, even if you have budgeted before, what factors can fluctuate from picture to picture? What budget items can never be predicted with certainty?

In general, I have learned to make a budget and then double it and the timeframe. Why? Investors always want to cut your budget and the timeframe. Knowing this, I might as well give them something to cut. I also have learned that I cannot predict the weather and downtime for temperamental actors and directors. Cash for unions dues, payroll taxes and the costs of permits can vary widely from film to film, but this information is easily available on websites, or can readily be provided by an experienced line producer.

A great budget will:

- Indicate how much money needs to be raised
- Control your expenditures
- Guide you in the right direction
- Keep you focused
- Evaluate alternative financing strategies

- Help you prepare for emergencies and large unanticipated expenses

Before you go out to raise money, you need to do your homework. You'll need to analyze your project in terms of cast, crew, locations, props and equipment. There's no magic secret to doing this quickly. You simply need to search the Internet and talk to your advisors to find out how much things cost. In addition, you'll make many phone calls to those in the industry who know.

Hopefully, during the course of all those phone calls, you'll make contacts and start to establish relationships with the people and businesses that will later become involved in your project. Many people are surprised to find out just how easy it can be to get a vendor to talk about their specialty and to provide quick estimates that will suffice for your preliminary budget.

Most beginners use spreadsheets or professional software, such as Movie Magic Budgeting.

The best way to research the budgets for the various departments in your production is to talk to the key person from that department. Talk to the Director of Photography about budgeting camera equipment, lighting and crew. Talk to the Editor about budgeting for editing. Talk to the Sound Designer about audio. Usually these people have a lot of experience and can give you quick answers about how long it usually takes to edit a feature film, how many people you'll need, and how many lighting packages you need for a night exterior shoot.

The next big item, after crew salaries, is equipment. Many low-budget producers must decide whether they want to purchase or rent equipment. To decide what's best for you, you'll have to consider the length of your shoot, the cost of the equipment and the potential for resale or re-use.

Often in the case of low-budget projects, it is more cost-effective to purchase equipment, such as cameras, non-linear editing equipment, computer, digital video tape decks and storage drives, than it is to rent it. This is especially true for a digital video project with a long production schedule, such as a feature length film or hour-long documentary.

Some types of equipment are usually better to rent than purchase. You'll want to rent things that you won't be using all the time or will be changing frequently such as lights, tripods and steadicam units, lighting accessories, and microphones. You'll also want to rent things that you could never afford to buy, such as expensive digital cameras (i.e., Red or Arriflex D-20) and digital video decks.

Some rental houses (like Panavision) are willing to give low-budget films and first-time directors a break and give you equipment as an in-kind donation; treating it as investment in your future business with them.

Many other expenses will arise during the course of your production: office supplies, faxing, cell phone bills, the cost of feeding the cast and crew, travel, and much more. These will vary greatly depending on your project, but be careful not to underestimate them.

"Contingency" is a sum you add to your budget in case of unforeseen expenses, such as a rainy day (literally) during your shoot, a sick actor, and so on. Most budgets add a fixed percentage for contingencies, which is usually 10 percent of the combined above-the-line and below-the-line budget.

Your contingency budget accounts for things that you cannot reasonably predict up front, such as your shoot going into overtime or additional production days. This extra time can cost quite a bit and will come out of the contingency budget. Additional war stories include hard drive crashes, special actor accommodations, unanticipated travel, set destruction, loss of film, shooting permits and the like. With over 20 people working on a project, something unanticipated is bound to happen.

Although this might seem a bit premature, it's wise to set up your production accounting early on. The easy way, of course, is to hire an accountant to work on your staff or contract an outside payroll service. But if your project is small, you may need to do the accounting yourself.

Once you've completed your research and filled out your preliminary budget, you'll need to create a budget top sheet. The budget top sheet (AKA summary) shows the subtotals for all the accounts in your budget and then the total budget. It's a simple, easy to read summary of your budget that you can include in proposals and pitches.

Once you've found your funding, you'll be able to revise your budget with a set dollar amount in mind.

Whether you choose to dedicate your entire funding amount to getting your project "in the can" or divvy up your funding between production and post-production, you'll have marks to hit as you go through your original preliminary budget. You'll also know what areas of your budget may be in jeopardy.

Be very realistic. Just because you want hot special effects doesn't mean you should get them at the expense of the other elements in your production. Spreading your resources too thin is a common mistake. One key mantra to abide by when revising a budget is to spend money that will be seen on screen. For if you shortchange these critical items, you will probably wind up with a film that looks amateurish.

For years, movies have featured real products instead of generic "cola" bottles. Such product placements were often paid for by sponsors but lingered in the background. Movies have become the new product showcases, as a shrinking ad market, climbing productioncosts, and ad-skipping technology lead producers to become more blatant about dropping product names into their projects.

Rather than existing as mere props, products are being woven more tightly into story lines as crucial plot points or subjects of dialogue.

If you plan to seek funds from product integration companies (who represent major advertisers), please add an additional sheet to your business plan identifying the types of products that would naturally weave into your storyline. Make sure to calculate the time on screen and the importance of the character holding or talking with the product in their hand.

Tax incentives can help influence where you make your film. We will discuss tax incentives in more detail later in the book.

The following items are typically budgeted for a small independent film:

>Story and Script
>Story Rights
>Writer and Screenplay
>Typing and Duplication
>
>Producer and Director
>Executive Producer
>Producer
>Director
>Expenses
>
>Star Performers
>Day Player Performers
>Extras
>Stunt persons
>Union Fees

Other

Production Staff
Production Manager
Assistant Director
Production Secretary
Script Supervisor
Production Assistants
Director of Photography
Camera Assistants
Gaffer
Best Boy
Key Grip
Dolly Grip
Electricians
Sound Mixer
Boom Operator
Production Designer/Art Director
Assistant Art Director
Property Master
Wardrobe Supervisor
Makeup Artist
Special Effects
Drivers/Teamsters

Still Photographer
Casting Director

Locations & Studio
Transportation
Per Diems
Petty Cash
Catering
Location Fees and Permits
Travel Expenses
Set Construction/Supplies

Production Equipment
Cameras
Filters
Sound Equipment
Lighting Equipment
Dolly & Grip Equipment
Other

Raw Stock
35 MM Negative
Audio Stock
Production Stills/Unit Photographer

Processing

Sound Transfers

Miscellaneous
Props
Wardrobe
Office and Phone
Postage/FedEx
Accounting
Legal
Insurance
Audition Expenses
Tests & Retakes
Publicity

Sound and Music
Composer
Stock Music and Sound Effects
Studio Costs
Foley/ADR
Sound Transfers
Mixing Theater

Editing and Finishing

Editor

Assistant Editor(s)

Sound Editor

Cutting Room Rental

Supplies

Coding

Main/End Titles

Opticals

Videos & Scratch Prints

Negative Cutting

Printing

Reels, Cans and Cases

Film-to-Tape Transfer

To get samples of movie budgets, you may want to join a professional organization that has an extensive research library or use the samples that come with professional budget software.

As you can see, there is a lot of work you need to do on your budget before you even think of preparing the final shooting draft of your script. And, often, you will find that you do not need to budget for certain items. Let experience be your guide.

If you are having difficulty with your budget, or are concerned about presenting a budget to a seasoned investor, consider hiring an experienced line producer to prepare your budget. I have found many good ones listed on IMDb.

The line producer is one of the first people to be employed on a film's production. Line producers are rarely involved in the development of the project, but often play a crucial role in determining the cost to provide investors with the confidence to invest in the project. As soon as the financing has been raised, the line producer supervises the preparation of the film's budget, and the day-to-day planning and running of the production.

Line producers are usually recruited onto the production team during the later stages of development. They can be highly instrumental in successfully achieving the creative vision of the project at a stage when changes and revisions in the script are inexpensive to make. In addition, an experienced line producer has a wealth of knowledge that can positively affect the final outcome of the project, and lead to a successful production.

The line producer takes the script and assesses the likely below-the-line cost of the production by breaking down the screenplay into a schedule (a timetable for the film shoot that shows how long it will take to shoot each scene). From this schedule, the line producer can accurately estimate the cost of each day's shooting and produce a provisional budget estimating the total amount of funding required. Once you have raised funds, the film can go into pre-production.

Experienced line producers possess in-depth knowledge of scheduling and budgeting, and of all the physical and technical processes of filmmaking. They must have excellent industry contacts and must command the respect of the production crew. Exceptional communication skills are required, as well as diplomatic skills to balance the creative expectations of the director, artists and creative personnel with the financial resources available.

Chapter 11
Hollywood Accounting

Traditionally, large studios use Hollywood accounting to distribute profits earned on a mega-hit movie to corporate entities, which they own. This has the net result of reducing the project's reported profit by a substantial margin, sometimes even eliminating it altogether. Although this may be for income tax purposes, it is often used to reduce the amount studios have to pay in royalties and profit-sharing agreements to third parties such as A-list actors, directors and producers.

Since I deal only with independent movies, my goal is to get my investors and myself the maximum return for our investment. We recognize the risk that we must take and know what returns we require in order to get investors interested in our projects.

I look over every budget and try to determine whether overhead charges are reasonable:

Production overhead - a lump sum assigned by the studio to support a motion picture project. I do not like large producer fees and items called miscellaneous.

Distribution overhead - a negotiated amount with a film distributor who will distribute the picture to various local and international markets, including theater, DVD, television and airlines. I do not like large numbers for print and advertising.

Marketing overhead - a lump sum to promote the picture in ads, posters, events, festivals and the like. I question items for excess travel, lodging and meals.

Obviously, the ideal goal is to make a picture and sell it to a distributor for a fixed amount. This way the filmmaker locks in his/her profits. Unfortunately, if the movie becomes a mega hit, the filmmaker and investors leave money on the table.

In today's market, an independent filmmaker may have to share profits with a distributor in order to get their attention. No one wants to be sitting on expensive inventory which cannot be sold.

For 70 plus years, Hollywood studios have abused accounting rules to maximize accounting losses to mask the profitability of a breakout blockbuster.

Hollywood studios are masters at using magic and it is extremely rare for anyone to succeed against a well-funded organization loaded with "kill-or-be-killed" accountants and lawyers.

In addition, suing for what is rightfully yours will backfire and sabotage your future endeavors. You reputation as a non-player will be tarnished, and you will be branded as an "overly litigious" person. Rumors will spread that you are "difficult to work with."

Everyone assumed that I would become a CPA. Grandpa Charlie and my father, who worked for Grandpa right out of college, were CPAs. As I grew up, they took me to the office during tax season. I would make copies of tax returns for clients and file them in a labor-intensive cross-referenced system. I still remember getting filthy hands running the Bruning machine, which made copies of tax returns for clients, partners and the file room. On the other hand, I also remember eating lunch with all these old people who shared how much money they were making, as I looked over Wall Street from the 40th floor of a New York City office building.

When I was older, and somewhat experienced from my teen years, they expected me to work for a major accounting firm. So, after graduate school and four years at Citibank, I worked for Peat Marwick Mitchell, one of the former Big 8 national accounting firms. Ironically, I never learned Movie Accounting at the Big 8; what I did learn was how the world of global finance operated.

I saw how money was made and moved around the world. It fascinated me that millions of dollars would be made in the US and invested in other countries only to be brought back with huge foreign exchange gains. At Citibank, I learned how to hedge foreign exchange gains.

At Peat, I learned how to account and shelter those gains through legitimate tax shelters.

Once I realized that I enjoyed research and did well at it, clients wanted me to research topics, which would help them either accelerate accounting revenues in order to boost earnings per share (EPS) or decrease taxable revenues in order to lower corporate income taxes. When I could accomplish both at the same time, I was considered a "boy genius."

Accounting and tax abuses have been around for thousands of years. It is human nature to "milk" the system and a select few intelligentsias (i.e., Goldman Sachs) will always try to game the system in their favor.

History shows that companies are capable of showing paper profits because of bookkeeping tricks. Although it requires intelligence to beat the system, it also requires the power to do so.

For a hundred years, corporate accounting had an 'anything goes' policy. There were no rules, only GAAP. Corporate management hired accountants to serve their needs, not the public. That meant that, in practice, the primary function of accounting was to make management look good.

For your reading pleasure, here are some of the top Hollywood Accounting rip-offs:

"Chicago: The Musical" - Producer Martin Richards sold Miramax an option to the movie rights to the musical in 1994. In papers filed in New York State Supreme Court, he said that he has been cheated out of $10 million in profits due to underreporting of revenues. Court papers said that his contract called for him to be paid several fees, including $500,000 after the movie reached its initial break-even point. The film, which opened in December 2002, starred Richard Gere, Catherine Zeta-Jones and Renee Zellweger and won six Academy Awards, including one for best picture. The court papers said that the film was budgeted at $47 million and went over budget by about $10 million. The lawsuit claims that "Chicago" was the highest-grossing film ever released by the studio and that the movie generated gross receipts of about $300 million, including $170 million during its initial domestic release, and many millions more from DVD, video and foreign distribution.

"Coming to America" - Buchwald v. Paramount (1990) was a breach of contract lawsuit filed in California in which humorist and writer Art Buchwald alleged that Paramount Pictures stole his script idea and turned it into the 1988 movie "Coming to America." Buchwald won the lawsuit, was awarded damages, and then accepted a settlement from Paramount before any appeal took place. The decision was important mainly for the court's determination in the penalty phase of the trial that Paramount used "unconscionable" means of determining how much to pay authors. Paramount claimed, and provided accounting evidence to support the claim, that despite the movie's US$350 million in revenues, it had earned no net profit, according to the definition of "net profit" in Buchwald's contract, and hence Buchwald was owed nothing.

"JFK - The Movie" - The class-action antitrust lawsuit was filed by the heirs of Jim Garrison, whose book "On the Trail of the Assassin" was the foundation of the 1991 Oliver Stone film "JFK." According to the suit, Warner Bros. says that the movie has not earned any money under the studio's "net profits" accounting formula. The assassination-conspiracy film grossed more than $150 million worldwide, according to the lawsuit. But the estate of Mr. Garrison has not received any profit participation income, to which it is contractually entitled.

"My Big Fat Greek Wedding" - In yet another lawsuit challenging Hollywood's accounting practices, Tom Hanks, his wife Rita Wilson, and writer-actress Nia Vardalos sued Gold Circle Films, claiming the company has cheated them out of millions of dollars. The lawsuit, filed in Los Angeles, claimed that their film grossed about $370 million, while the studio indicated its gross receipts totaled $287 million.

"Lord of the Rings" - Peter Jackson's dispute with New Line Cinema was settled for $40 million after a long, drawn out battle. Peter Jackson's claim was launched in 2005 when he claimed the studio had miscalculated his share of receipts from the "Lord of the Rings" trilogy. In his lawsuit, Mr. Jackson claimed that New Line committed fraud in its handling of the revenues. Jackson had claimed that he was underpaid by as much as $100 million for the trilogy. In addition, J.R.R. Tolkien sold the movie rights to his "Lord of the Rings" novels 40 years ago for 7.5 percent of future receipts. Three films and $6 billion later, his heirs say they haven't seen a dime from

Time Warner. They recently settled for an undisclosed amount.

Since no studio head or corporate executive wants to be subpoenaed in a lawsuit over accounting, vertical integration lawsuits are usually settled before reaching open court.For more details on Hollywood Accounting Case Studies please visit:

http://showbizmanagementadvisors.com

Chapter 12

What Makes a Great Movie?

Most movies are written in the traditional three-act structure that the Greeks mastered over 2500 years ago, as organized and specifically laid out in Aristotle's *Poetics* and developed with respect to feature films by Syd Field, author of *Screenplay: The Foundations of Screenwriting* and *The Screen Writer's Workbook*. The three acts are *set up* (the location and characters), *confrontation* (obstacle) and *resolution* (culmination into a climax and dénouement.) In a two-hour film, the first and third acts typically last 30 minutes, while the middle act lasts an hour.

"The Hero's Journey" is an idea formulated by noted mythologist Joseph Campbell. The central concept is that a universal pattern can be seen in stories and myths across history and cultures. Campbell defined and explained this pattern in his book, *The Hero with a Thousand Faces* (1949). This book is required reading, along with Christopher Volger's *The Screenwriter's Journey* and Blake Snyder's *Save The Cat*.

Campbell's insight showed that important worldwide myths, which have survived for thousands of years, all share a fundamental structure. This fundamental structure contains a number of stages, including:

- A call to adventure, which the hero has to accept or decline.
- A road of trials, on which the hero succeeds or fails.
- Achieving the goal or "boon" which often results in important self-knowledge.
- A return to the ordinary world, in which the hero can succeed or fail.
- Application of the boon, in which what the hero has gained can be used to improve the world.

So, with all of the major studio talent behind the greenlighting of movie projects, how come Hollywood has a less than perfect score for identifying winners on a consistent basis?

According to Jehoshua Eliashberg, Sam K. Hui, and Z. John Zhang of The Wharton School of Finance at the University of Pennsylvania, movie studios often have to choose among thousands of scripts to decide which ones to turn into movies. Despite the huge amount of money at stake, this process, known as "greenlighting," is largely guesswork based on experts' experience and intuitions.

Despite the market size and investment interests, new movie production is a risky venture and profitability varies greatly across movies. While producers sometimes make large amounts of profit from blockbusters, they also lose millions of dollars in movies that end up in oblivion.

For example, "Gigli" cost $54 million to produce, but generated only $6 million at the box office. Considering that studios generally receive a share of around 50% of the gross box-office revenue for their production, Gigli generated a ROI of -96.7% for the studio.

On the other end of the spectrum, although the movie "In the Bedroom" cost only $1.7 million to produce and generated more than $35 million in box-office revenues, it produced a ROI of +667%.

Across a sample of 281 movies produced between 2001 and 2004, studios' ROI ranged from -96.7% to over 677%, with a median of -27.2%. Note that the negative median implies that there is a high probability of movies losing money for their investors.

Deciding which scripts to produce is a dauntingly difficult task. Each year it has been estimated that more than 15,000 screenplays are registered with the Writers Guild of America (WGA), while only around 700 movies are made, which is less than 5%. Thus, studios need a more reliable approach to greenlight films.

For years, the major studios have employed an age-old, labor-intensive methodology: they hire "readers" to assist them in evaluating screenplays.

It is my experience that most readers are young, naive, self-centered and have no concept of reality beyond Hollywood, and their own star-struck tastes, frustrated dreams and cynical points-of-view work against them. Hollywood is a notorious town where top-level people "don't read" crucial material until there's enough "buzz" about the project from other sources that they trust. Therefore, the gatekeepers (i.e., readers) inhibit most great scripts from getting to the right people.

Typically, one to three readers or other development personnel are assigned to read each script. After a reader reads a script, he/she writes a synopsis of the storyline and makes an initial recommendation ("the coverage") on whether the screenplay should be produced into a movie and the changes, if any, that are needed before actual pre-production can start.

This approach becomes especially problematic when disagreements among readers and studio executives occur. Even the scripts for highly successful movies, such as "Star Wars" and "Raiders of the Lost Ark," were initially bounced around at several studios before Twentieth Century-Fox and Paramount picked them up.

Based on extensive industry research, there are 22 criteria for determining the success of a movie:

- Clear Premise: The story has a clear premise that is important to audiences.

- Familiar Setting: The setting of the story is familiar to you.
- Early Exposition: Information about characters comes very early in the story.
- Coincidence Avoidance: Story follows a logical, causal relationship.
- Inter-Connected: Each scene description advances the plot and is closely connected to the central conflict.
- Surprise: The story contains elements of surprise, but is logical within context and within its own rules.
- Anticipation: Keeps viewers trying to anticipate what will happen next.
- Flashback Minimization: Flashbacks amplify reasons for character behaviors.
- Linear Timeline: The story unfolds in chronological order.
- Clear Motivation: The hero of the story has a clear outer motivation (what he/she wants to achieve by the end of the movie).
- Multi-dimensional Hero: Many dimensions of the hero are explored.
- Strong Nemesis: There is a strong nemesis in the story.
- Sympathetic Hero: Hero attracts your sympathy because he/she exhibits courage and is nice, funny,

or good at what he does or has a power which we envy.

- Logical Characters: Actions of main characters are logical considering their characteristics. They sometimes hold surprises, but are believable.
- Character Growth: Conflict is important enough to change the hero.
- Important Conflict: The story has a very clear conflict, which involves high emotional stakes.
- Multi-Dimensional Conflict: The central conflict is explained in many different points of view.
- Conflict Build-up: The hero faces a series of hurdles. Each successive hurdle is greater and more provocative than the previous ones.
- Conflict Lock-in: The hero is locked into the conflict very early in the movie.
- Unambiguous Resolution: Conflict is clearly resolved through confrontation between the hero and nemesis at the end.
- Logical Ending: The ending is logical and believable.
- Surprise Ending: The ending carries surprise and is unexpected.

Although deviating from this formula may be attractive, business investors do not like to take chances. They prefer to stay with proven formulas. And even then, they can still lose their entire investment due to creative changes during the filmmaking process.

Chapter 13
Isolating Investment Risk Through Limited Liability Corporations (LLCs)

Although there are many corporate structures to choose from, many production companies choose to create LLCs to account for production company activities. This is true whether a producer is making a short film or creating a larger feature film project involving hundreds of thousands of dollars, salaried employees, and a crew of independent contractors.

The goal of creating and using a business entity anticipates four primary areas: control, financing, liability and tax.

Control refers to the manner in which a producer intends to manage and maintain control of the film project. It involves issues such as "Who owns the film's intellectual property?" and "Who has the right to manage the creative, financial and business aspects of the film project?"

Financing refers to the source of funding for the film including interactions with equity investors. Liability refers to the obligations incurred by the film production and the producer's personal liability for such obligations. Tax refers to the tax benefits and tax obligations incurred in the production and distribution of the film.

The most common business entities are sole proprietorships, general partnerships, corporations and limited liability companies. The first two types (sole proprietorships and general partnerships) should not be used in film production because they expose the producer to individual liability for the debts of the production. This is particularly true because independent film projects normally take at least 3 years (and often 5 or more years) to reach the production phase and it may take another 2 years to obtain a meaningful distribution deal (that is, a deal where money flows back to you).

Keep in mind that film production is a very high-risk endeavor and individual liability will expose you to the demands of creditors who want to be paid today. Thus, it is well worth the time and expense of forming a company and conducting all business in corporate form.

By organizing and operating as a corporation or a limited liability company, a producer can avoid personal liability for the business's operations and can more easily bring investors into the project. Remember that corporate protection may disappear if you fail to comply with all the formalities.

For example, if you fail to file annual reports with the Secretary of State, your company will be dissolved, or if you mix personal and company funds, creditors may be able to reach your personal assets. So, create a separate bank account and federal tax ID for your operating entities.

To determine which entity is best for your project, you should speak with an accountant, attorney or someone familiar with the benefits and burdens of each type of entity. Setting up a corporation or LLC is a relatively simple process that involves filing certain forms with your State.

Please be careful about setting up an entity in Nevada or Delaware. Many companies do this due to those states' lack of corporate tax rules. Many, however, are unaware that they may have to travel there to present arguments in lawsuits, racking up thousands of dollars in travel and lodging expenses.

When developing a film project, many producers first create an incubator corporation or LLC (the "Development Company") that develops one or more projects until the time when each project is ready to be funded and produced. The Development Company, which is controlled by the producer, does all the development work for the film project, such as acquiring the underlying literary work or screenplay on which the film is based. When the project is ready for funding and production, it is transferred to a separate LLC (the "Production LLC"); the common practice being to create a separate LLC for each film project, thus insulating the producer's other projects from failure or liability. The Development Company often serves as the manager of the Production LLC, thus creating a double level of protection for the individual producer.

A Production LLC will own or license all of the intellectual property associated with the film. This includes the rights to use the script, the rights to the actor's performances, and licenses for all music. Potential distributors will carefully examine all of the Production LLC's paperwork to make sure that the Production LLC holds all necessary intellectual property rights. Anyone working on the production should be hired by and paid by the Production LLC.

A Limited Liability Company (LLC) is a business structure allowed by state statute. LLCs are popular, because similar to a corporation, owners have limited personal liability for the debts and actions of the LLC. Other features of LLCs are more like a partnership, providing management flexibility and the benefit of pass-through taxation.

The LLC allows for multiple owners, or members, who enjoy limited liability, as well as a managing member, who also enjoys limited liability and typically is the person responsible for managing the business.

Profits or losses of the business pass directly through to the owner's personal income tax return, Form 1040. The LLC files a Form 1065, and then lists each member's taxable profit on Form K-1. The bottom-line profit of the business is not considered to be earned income to the members, and therefore is not subject to self-employment tax.

Owners of an LLC are called members. Because most states don't restrict ownership, members may include individuals, corporations, other LLCs and foreign entities. There is no maximum number of members. Most states also permit "single member" LLCs, which are those having only one owner.

I encourage moviemakers to set up LLCs for their projects and track their business expenses for tax purposes. Do not commingle your personal and your corporate funds, because the IRS will disallow your business deductions if they don't think you're regularly attending to the business matters at hand.

Although I prefer Internet-provided forms, it's OK to use paper forms. In fact, LegalZoom.com is easy, fast and a comprehensive way to set up your LLC. In Arizona, I use online systems to first check to see if the LLC name is available and reserve it before I file the necessary paperwork. This way, no one can come along and snatch my idea.

In addition, I try to set up multiple LLCs for various transactions in order to insulate any one business or activity from taking down the entire business.

Most people pitch their projects as part of an LLC in order to minimize the risk to the writer/producer. However, by transferring all of the risk to an investor, the moviemaker inadvertently forces the investor to look at the possibility of losing all of their investment.

The business landscape is littered with would-be moviemakers who have stumbled in their search for funding. Many requests are denied. Those who pass the test frequently have unacceptable strings attached. Some deals that close come back to bite the moviemaker in the form of onerous debt, insufficient profit sharing and personal liability.

Part of the problem lies in the nature of the startup endeavor. Freshly minted moviemakers, who may lack business experience and collateral to secure investors, pose major risks to potential investors. Family, friends, banks, venture capital firms and angel investors are not interested in losing their investment.

Chapter 14
What Makes a Great Business Plan?

I have started many companies in my life. Many have succeeded and many have failed. Even when I failed, I learned something that would help me prevail on my next project.

Many experts tell you to write a business plan. I think they are a waste of time since they try to predict the future, which is an impossible endeavor. However, investors need to see something in writing. No one is going to give you millions of dollars without some form of written strategy and comprehensive competitive analysis.

As you start to create your business plan, do not sweat the details. They can always be filled in later. Make sure you develop a strong framework that makes sense to you and your potential investors.

Your business plan needs to cover The Market, Market Segmentation, Consumer Analysis, Competition, Product Features and Benefits, Competitive Analysis, Positioning, Advertising and Promotion, Sales, Research and Development, Operations, Creative & Business People, Payback/Exit Plan and Financial Projections.

Great business plans follow a tried-and-true format, which investors recognize. Deviate from this format and your creativity can jeopardize your ability to raise money for your project. Highlight key concepts in separate sections so that an investor can immediately flip to the section he wants to review.

Some investors love numbers. Others want to see what actors are attached; while many look at marketing strategies. Make it simple to find the answers in the details.

Many business plans are divided into seven sections as follows:
- Executive Summary
- Company Summary
- Description of Movie Project
- Market Analysis
- Strategy and Implementation Analysis
- Management Summary
- Financial Plan

Start with a good template. There are many on the Internet. There are some free ones at SCORE, a federal agency funded by the Small Business Administration.

Your business plan must consist of a coherent, clean and concise narrative and expert financial worksheets. Write from the heart. Get your thoughts on paper. Do not edit the first time. You can always edit after you have totally exhausted your thoughts.

The real value of creating a business plan is that it forces you to research and think about your movie in a systematic way. Planning helps you to think things through thoroughly, hopefully avoiding costly mistakes later.

Pay particular attention to your writing style. You will be judged by the quality and appearance of your work as well as by your ideas.

It typically takes several weeks to complete a good plan. Most of that time is spent in research and re-thinking your ideas and assumptions. So take as much time as you need to do the job properly.

Here are some key questions that you need to answer in your business plan:

What is the purpose of your movie?

What background experience, skills and strengths do you personally bring to this new venture?

Who will your customers be?

What are your customers' characteristics?

Why do your customers need to see your movie?

How do you plan to market your movie?

Who is on your management team?

What previous successes have been attributed to your team members?

What competition do you face?

What do you think the future holds for independent films?

If you are looking for money, state clearly how much you want, precisely how you are going to use it, and how the money will make your movie more profitable, thereby ensuring repayment. Be open and honest. Tell investors how long it is going to take to give them back their money and what ROI they can expect.

Many financing efforts fail because of avoidable mistakes that you can make when you pitch potential investors, structure agreements and manage money once the deal is done.

For example:

Half-baked business plans - There's nothing worse than going into a money meeting unprepared. If you haven't put the time and energy into writing a full-blown business plan complete with elements, such as a cogent business description, financial projections and a competitive market analysis, the people with the cash will not put the time into evaluating your proposal.

Focusing too much on the idea and too little on management - It's not enough to convince potential backers that you've written a great movie. You also need a team that can generate the revenues to repay a bank loan or provide an exit strategy for a VC or angel investor. Many business novices ignore the second part of the equation.

The greatest racehorse in the world still needs a great jockey to a win a race. The same principle applies in business. Showing that you have attached quality talent, an experienced director and a willing distributor is essential to winning over investors.

Not asking for enough money - In a 2004 US Bank study of "Reasons for Small Business Failures," 79 percent cited "starting out with too little money" as one of the top causes of their collapse and subsequent failure. This is because entrepreneurs who are wet behind the ears don't realize that they need to calculate their borrowing needs based on their worst-case scenario instead of their best-case forecast. Operating with the worst-case scenario mindset in the first three years forces you to address needs, situations and events with a more practical and realistic outlook.

An old accounting axiom says, "Everything will take twice as long and cost twice as much as you expect." Inexperienced filmmakers tend to be overly optimistic about how soon they will begin to fill their cash pipeline and how fast the money will flow. If you're underfunded, you won't have a cushion to tide you over in the event of slow initial sales or unexpected market conditions.

Having too many lenders or investors - one of the hazards of securing financing from multiple sources is managing too many relationships and expectations. It takes time away from your core business. These not-so-silent partners may have conflicting agendas, self-interests and demands with devastating consequences. This is particularly true when you raise money from friends and family.

Failing to get the proper legal agreements - every lender or investor eventually will need his or her money back, and a legal document covering everything from the terms to the timing can avoid acrimony among your investors.

Poor cash flow management - Too many moviemakers burn through their seed money too quickly and fail to reach cash flow-positive status in a timely manner. Some causal factors, such as budget overruns and economic downturns may be beyond one's control, but the executive team is clearly at fault for others, such as unnecessary spending and overly optimistic expense/income forecasts. Financial sponsors don't take kindly to that sort of mismanagement. And if they turn off the tap, all of your hard work goes down the drain.

Many movies fail to attract investors, especially during tough economic downturns. Ironically, this is the best time to make a film, since there is very little competition for investment dollars. On top of that, costs are lower, and more talent is available, thanks to a shortage of good paying projects.

If you are writing a business plan, then you need to write a clear and convincing business plan. Anything less is heading straight for the wastebasket. The intended recipients of such business plans—investors and lenders, family and friends, anyone with capital to invest in the project—are all much more wary of risk now in these turbulent times.

Most business plans fail to impress potential investors. Most aren't even read in full. Their shortcomings tend to be obvious because the people seeking money have not done their homework. Plans fail because the writer misses selling the point. Here are some examples from plans that I have read over the years:

The writer is self-absorbed with the elegance of his or her technology. The plan begins not with the identification of a customer problem to resolve, but with a detailed explanation of how the technology works, why it is cutting-edge or state-of-the-art, and how it is better, faster and cheaper than current solutions.

The writer rests his case on a truckload of data to show how large and fast-growing a market is. The plan then makes a heroic leap and assumes that the new venture will grab X percent of that market—it could be 1%, 10%, 30% or whatever. "Surely," the plan argues, "With the large number of customers going to the movies, we'll easily get enough."

The writer offers detailed spreadsheets showing why the numbers would work. Savvy investors not only tear apart the spreadsheets, but ask fundamental questions. Does the revenue model depend on making a large number of small transactions (think Amazon.com) or a small number of large ones (automobile manufacturing)? Do its profit margins depend on high gross margins to cover high product-development costs (think Microsoft), or lower margins to cover slimmer operating costs (Costco)?

Investors won't be snowed by top-tier diplomas or past employment with a leading company. Investors care first about the main challenges of the film industry in question, and whether the proposed team has hands-on experience tackling those challenges.

Every industry has critical success factors—typically two or three—that, when addressed effectively, are likely to bring success even if less-important challenges aren't handled well. A business plan that identifies its critical success factors and shows how the team's expertise and experience are suited to addressing them is much more likely to attract capital—or at least a second look.

Surprisingly, plans that point out the lack of a key skill or capability in the management team can fare quite well, by acknowledging the missing link and encouraging the prospective investor to fill that slot with a qualified person whom he or she favors. Plans that succeed in attracting capital often include one or more members of a team who have failed in a prior venture. When that failure is accompanied by lessons learned, it's often viewed as an education on someone else's nickel.

The most common type of business plan, and the one that goes most quickly into the trash, is the one in which the writer can't find anything but good things to say about the opportunity and plans to pursue it. Investors know that in the real world, most opportunities, even good ones, have some weaknesses. Most industries are not filled with infinite possibilities, especially given the overcapacity in today's global economy. Experienced entrepreneurs know better than to assert that everything is wonderful about their opportunity. They know there are potential pitfalls in their market or industry. The facts are that most opportunities are highly uncertain. Most new ventures will fail. Of the few that do succeed, candor is key.

According to Rosalind Resnick, she believes that business plans may be irrelevant, obsolete and a conspiracy by consultants and business schools to take advantage of inexperienced entrepreneurs with more dollars than sense.

After all, who needs to write a 50-page term paper or build a complex financial model in Excel, when a start-up like Twitter can launch a web site, command a billion-dollar valuation from top venture capitalists and figure out how it's going to make money after it gets funded? In fact, a 2007 survey conducted by Babson College of 116 businesses launched by its alumni between 1985 and 2003 found no statistical difference between the success achieved by those businesses that started with a formal business plan and those that forged ahead without one. The only companies that really need a business plan, Babson's researchers concluded, are businesses seeking to "raise external start-up capital from institutional sources or business angels."

So, if you're financing your own film, have no staff, overhead or inventory, you probably don't need to waste your time or money on a formal business plan. However, no film can be made without the use of other media professionals such as cameramen, makeup, actors and the like. As a result, even a small business plan will do better than none at all.

Now I'm not suggesting that, just because your company needs a business plan, you need to hire a high-priced MBA or consultant to write it for you. What I am advising is that you take the time to map out your strategy with well-researched words and numbers, so that you can figure out for yourself where you want your film project to go and how you're going to get there.

Business Plan Checklist

by
Jeffrey Taylor

Overview of Business Plan Format

(1) Investor Cover Letter
(2) Project One Sheet (Mock-up of Poster)
(3) Offering Summary
(4) Executive One Sheet
(5) Project Information Form
(6) Budget Top Sheet
(7) Cash Flow Schedule
(8) Market Projections
(9) Market Comparables
(10) Talent Sheet
(11) Producer Term Sheet
(12) Developmental Budget
(13) Summary of Flow of Funds
(14) Industry Risk Factors
(15) Distribution Models
(16) Manager/Producer and Key Personnel Biographies
(17) Company Operating Agreement of LLC
(18) Single Purpose Producing Entity Formation Documents

(19) Investor Subscription Booklet
(20) Investor Side-letter to Subscription Agreement
(21) Defined Proceeds Definition
(22) Executive Producer Agreement
(23) Sales Agency Agreement
(24) Filming Incentive Estimates
(25) Escrow Agreement
(26) Producer Draw Down Schedule

Timelines of Producer, Directors, Actors and Distribution

(1) The Development Timeline and Production Schedule
(2) Attaching a Producer
(3) Producer Agreements
(4) Producer Guild of America
(5) The Director Agreement
(6) Casting and Agency Relations
(7) The Proposed Cast List
(8) The Casting Director
(9) Identifying the Principal and Major Supporting Cast Members
(10) Cast Offers and What the Market Will Bear
(11) Cast Escrow Financing Agreements
(12) Talent Services Agreements, Client Escrows and Pay or Play Offers
(13) Prepping the Agent, their Client Actor and Making the Cast Offer
(14) Attaching the Actor

Prepping Your Project for Financing the Production Budget

(1) Budgeting and Schedules
(2) Bankers and Bank Lender Models and Requirements
(3) Film Incentives and Estimating the Soft Money Recoupment
(4) Foreign Estimates and Pre-Sale Valuations
(5) Collateralizing the Marketplace
(6) Determining the Equity Financing Requirement
(7) Budget Financing Scenarios
(8) Choosing the Filming Locations
(9) State Incentive Applications
(10) Mortgage and Assignment of Copyright Agreements
(11) Bonding the Production
(12) Circulating the Executive One Sheet
(13) US Distributor Tracking
(14) Prepping Your Production Funding and Your Equity Investors
(15) Determining the Principal Photography Start Date and Final Production Schedule
(16) Production Draw Down and Schedule

The Final Information Package & Financing Your Project

(1) The Final Production "Information Package"
(2) The Final Development Budget
(3) The Final Production Budget and Financing Plan
(4) Press Announcements
(5) Executive Producer Agreements
(6) Confidentiality and Non-Disclosure Agreements
(7) Investor Relations
(8) Like-Minded Investors
(9) Sharing Information with Investors and Timing
(10) General Rules of Raising Money
(11) Conflicts of Interest
(12) Financial Legal Affairs
(13) The Production Funding Timeline and Equity Offering Period
(14) Securing Production Funds and Funding Operations

Note : Not all sections need to be completed for all films

The bottom line is this: Play by Investors' Rules to get them to open their checkbook, but protect yourself at the same time. There's no point in filming a movie that will eventually sink under the weight of your investors' demands. If your business plan is good enough and you approach the right people, you should be able to get your funding.

Chapter 15

Financing Alternatives

Over the last several years, cash poured in from DVDs. As a result, Hollywood was able to lure money from outside investors, such as banks and hedge funds. However, many of these films disappointed at the box office, leaving investors with poor returns. As a result, financing is harder to come by. And, in some cases, has dried up altogether.

Until your film funds itself, you'll always be looking for money to get your project done and marketed to the public. Remember to raise money before you need it, because when you really need it, you'll find that there's no money to be had. That's just how life is.

It is my experience that there are five ways to raise money for your film; Friends & Family, Banks, Wall Street, Product Placement and Tax Incentives.

In this chapter, we will discuss the first four alternatives. Later in the book, we'll look at the most popular tax incentives.

Friends & Family

According to Entrepreneur Magazine, it has never been easy to raise capital for your small business (think of your independent movie project as a small business), especially if you are in the start-up phase. If you can't finance your project out of your own pocket, by maxing out your credit cards or taking out a home equity loan, you'll have to seek funding from the people who know and love you.

First, the good news: Friends and family members are more willing to invest in you because they love you. They are less likely to scrutinize every comma and semicolon in your business plan, or to demand a high return on their investment.

Now, the bad news. Raising money from friends and family creates personal and emotional issues that go beyond business judgment. If you borrow $10,000 from your family and fail to pay it back, you will have to deal with them the rest of your life.

I remember borrowing money from my parents, sister and ex-wife early in my career as an entrepreneur. It was great when I paid them back and terrible when I did not. Sad to say, but they rarely remembered the successes and always remembered the failures.

Aside from personal embarrassment, there are some real risks in taking money from friends and family. Friends and family members will inevitably say they are "giving" you money for your business, but rarely do they mean to make you an outright gift in the legal sense.

Because friend/family investments are usually made in a very informal way, misunderstandings can occur about precisely what the friend or family member expects in return for their money. You may think it is a loan, which you will repay in time with interest. Your friend or family member, on the other hand, may think of it as an investment for which they will receive a 'piece of the action.'

Banks

Banks, such as HSBC, have substantial finance experience in all areas of the film and television industry as well as maintain established relationships with studios, distributors, and completion guarantors.

Bank financing is extremely attractive, but difficult to obtain for a newcomer or moviemaker trying to finance a small budget film.

Basically, bank financing bridges the gap between production disbursements and distribution revenues by lending against distributor receivables.

Typically, the minimum loan is $5 million and paid back within 6-18 months through a revolving line of credit.

Banks tend to like films with 'movie stars', producers with proven track records and distributors with worldwide connections.

In some cases, to minimize risk, they may require a completion bond from a company that will guarantee the completion of the movie.

Wall Street

After years of watching Wall Street firms dump their own cash into principal investments, many of the nation's banks and investment banks spent trillions of their clients' money on financing motion picture projects.

In 2007, at the height of the Hollywood Investment craze, one of the most conservative financing institutions, J.P. Morgan, hired former Sony Pictures Entertainment executives Alan Levine and Ken Lemberger to head up a new unit called Entertainment Advisors to provide strategic and financial advice to clients in the entertainment business. The entertainment group invested its own capital and injected subordinated debt into nearly a dozen transactions. J.P. Morgan's investment bank also made a significant equity investment in Vine Alternative Investments, an entertainment fund.

Other major Wall Street bankers bankrolled studios by arranging loans for movie powerhouses DreamWorks, Revolution Studios, and New Line Cinema.

Wall Street never cared about movie plots. It was always about the money. Wall Street never read scripts, did not care about storylines, and never worried about which stars signed on, as long as they promised to work within the investor-approved budgets. Key concerns for Wall Street investors included the business plan, budget, release date, genre, and distribution schedule.

In fact, Wall Street came to believe that they could make money on any film project as long as there was enough marketing money and fame behind the project. Failure was never considered.

To minimize risk, Wall Street issued loans for slates of films at a given studio -- 5 to 15 at a time -- not single projects. They figured that 3 of 10 movies would do well and one would hit the jackpot, offsetting losses from the flops.

In late 2006, Tom Cruise and producing partner Paula Wagner were put in charge of United Artists, a film studio that was formed nearly 90 years ago by Hollywood actors Charlie Chaplin and Mary Pickford. Wagner would serve as chief executive of the company, which was owned by MGM.

The development was a major comeback for Cruise and Wagner. They were unceremoniously dismissed in August of 2006 from their 14-year producing deal at Paramount Studios after Sumner Redstone, chairman of Paramount parent company Viacom Inc., blamed

Cruise's public antics for hurting the box-office performance of "Mission: Impossible III." One could even argue that Cruise's public antics regarding his marriage to Katie Holmes and the public blowback still has lingering effects on his box-office appeal.

Two years later, struggling investment bank Merrill Lynch examined its contract with United Artists—Tom Cruise's production company—to determine whether it could revise the deal on better terms. United Artists had secured $500 million in financing from Merrill to fund 15 to 18 movies over the next five years.

Merrill was subsequently concerned about Paula Wagner's abrupt departure, after having greenlit two failures, "Lions for Lambs" and "Valkyrie," that both happened to star Tom Cruise; perhaps signaling the end of his leading man status among the movie-going public.

Finally, in 2008, the US economy started to tank, which brought the big banks to their knees (Merrill Lynch collapsed and was folded into Bank of America) and the highflying days of movie-finance investment banker moguls disappeared, taking a plentiful source of film finance away from new and established moviemakers.

Product Placement

Disney never makes a movie until they can figure out a way to market the success of the movie throughout their various co-owned product integration companies and businesses. Disney CEO Robert Iger has made this point well known.

They never miss a beat when it comes to merchandising, and that's never been more evident than with "The Princess and the Frog," released in December 2009.

From MP3 players, to apparel & jewelry, to beauty products, the movie stood on the cusp of history as Disney introduced its first Black princess. For the beauty line, they created a grooming set that included shampoo, conditioner, hair detangler and bubble bath from natural beauty line Carol's Daughter.

According to trade journals, Disney Consumer Products pitched the story for two years after brainstorming with animators on which products would make money for Disney, including fashion and home, toys, food, health and beauty, publishing and Disney Store exclusives.

All animated films push the usual product suspects, but Disney was inspired when it came to tie-ins. There is a doll for almost every outfit Tiana wears; Band-Aids; a reusable shopping tote; and a "blanket with sleeves," among many other things. There's even a cookbook (Princess Tiana shares a dream with her father to open a restaurant in New Orleans) with recipes for kids that include "Tiana's Famous Beignets" re-created from the film.

Tiana dances to her own beat, which includes a soundtrack that's a romp through the music closely associated with New Orleans, including musician Dr. John, who also voices a character in the film; jazz trumpet sensation and film score composer Terence Blanchard; and zydeco legend Terrance Simien.

Chapter 16

Film Distribution

We lived in Utah for 10 years and recently revisited the mall, which had a 10-plex cinema. We practically lived in the theater every Sunday morning, while others attended Church. They finally had to shut down the theater when it could not pay the land lease and property taxes.

Summer and Christmas season are Hollywood's two busy seasons, dominating the media chatter and the theater screens with blockbuster blowouts like "Transformers: Revenge of the Fallen" and "Inception." Fall, on the other hand, is the industry's serious season, when the Studios trot out the kind of aesthetically ambitious, modestly priced work that dominates Top 10 lists and tends to clean up at the Oscars.

In the last three years, however, several Studios have shut down or absorbed their specialty divisions that provided them with some of their most critically praised titles, films like "Good Night, and Good Luck" and "There Will Be Blood." Financing has dried up as the economy has gone sour, and even well-regarded films have struggled to turn a profit. All of which makes us wonder if these types of serious, middle-size movies will become an endangered species. And many Hollywood prognosticators, including myself, believe these films are on their way out, or destined for cable TV.

Yet, even as the ranks of studio divisions have thinned, the movies keep coming. In the past few years, the critics at *The New York Times* have reviewed more than 600 movies annually, sometimes 20 in a given week, a trend showing little signs of reversal. It isn't just big studio 3D releases that bring people into theaters. Business is brisk at boutique theaters like the IFC Center in Greenwich Village. And buying a ticket to stare at a screen in a room full of strangers is, of course, no longer the only way to see a movie. Distribution innovations, like video on demand (VOD), which can allow you to watch movies on your TV or iPhone the same day they open in theaters, have ushered in a new age of spectatorship.

A film distributor is an independent company, a subsidiary company, or an individual which acts as the final agent between a film production company and a film exhibitor, who secures placement of a producer's film on the exhibitor's screen.

The primary agenda of the distributor is to convince the exhibitor to rent or "book" each film. To this end, the distributor arranges industry screenings for exhibitors, and uses other marketing techniques that will show the exhibitor how he will profit financially by showing the film.

Once this is accomplished, the distributor then secures a written contract stipulating the amount of the gross ticket sales to be paid to the distributor (usually a percentage of the gross after first deducting a "floor" which is called a "house allowance"). The distributor then collects the amount due, audits the exhibitor's ticket sales as necessary to ensure the grosses are accurately reported by the exhibitor, secures the distributor's share of these proceeds, and transmits the remainder to the production company.

In addition, the distributor:
- ensures that enough film prints are made to service all contracted exhibitors on opening day
- ensures their physical delivery to the theater by the opening day
- monitors exhibitors to make sure the film is in fact shown in the particular theater with the minimum number of seats and show times
- ensures the prints' return to the distributor's office or other storage resource on the return date

In practical terms, this includes the physical production of film prints and the shipping of the prints around the world (a process that is beginning to be phased out by digital projection) as well as the creation of movie posters, newspaper and magazine advertisements, television commercials and trailers.

Furthermore, the distributor is responsible for ensuring a full line of film advertising material is available for each film, which the distributor believes will help the exhibitor attract the largest possible audience.

The distributor will create such advertising if it is not provided by the production company (in most cases the distributor will want to approve key art, trailers and other visual promotional elements) and arrange for the physical delivery of the advertising materials selected by the exhibitor prior to opening day.

If the distributor is handling an imported or foreign-language film, it may also be responsible for securing dubbing or subtitling for the film, and securing censorship or other legal or organizational "approval" for the exhibition of the film in the country/territory in which it does business.

The distributor wants to be able to have complete control of the dissemination of the filmed entertainment product that it is purchasing from the indie film producer, in order to exploit all forms of audience participation, such as cell phone, smartphone, VOD and DVD.

Can alternative media make up for lost box-office revenue? Subtitles and widescreen compositions don't look good on a cell phone, and the aesthetic and economic consequences of these new media are not yet proven.

Will the movie-going public continue in the age of the smartphone and the DVR? Will there be more movies or less?

Last year, the Academy Awards included 10 nominees for best picture, which was done to include more popular films. The big question is, "Do the Academy Awards actually matter?" Based on recent box-office receipts, there is no direct correlation between awards and receipts. People go for entertainment, even if the film only gets 1-star, such as the recent Stallone film, "Expendables."

Filmmaking is at a crossroads in terms of the manufacture and distribution of the product, because of out-of-balance global economics. Only time will tell how indie film survives in a tighter, stridently risk-adverse economic climate.

Chapter 17

Film Tax incentives

Congress imposed the first federal income tax in 1862 to finance the Civil War. It levied a 3% tax on incomes above $600, rising to 5% for incomes above $10,000. In 1895, the Supreme Court struck down the income tax, ruling that the portion of the income tax that applied to income on property was a direct tax that, under the US Constitution, could not be levied without apportioning the tax by population.

In 1913, the modern income tax system became possible when the states ratified the 16th Amendment to the US Constitution. That same year, the first Form 1040 appeared after Congress levied a 1% tax on net personal incomes above $3,000 with a 6% surtax on incomes of more than $500,000. As the nation sought greater revenue to finance the World War I effort, the top rate of income tax rose to 77% in 1918. It dropped sharply in the post-war years, down to 24% in 1929, and rose again during the Depression.

To combat alcohol abuse, Congress passed legislation to reduce crime and corruption, solve social problems, reduce the tax burden created by prisons and poorhouses, and improve health and hygiene in America.

During prohibition, Al Capone ruled Chicago with relentless power using Tommy gun-tinged assault tactics to quash rival gangsters. Ironically, brute strength and machine guns did not bring Capone to justice. Using the latest in criminology techniques, US Treasury Agent Eliot Ness arrested Capone for tax evasion.

The IRS discovered that Capone had not filed an income tax return for several years during which his lavish lifestyle suggested a very high income. Capone did not personally own bank accounts, sign checks or own any assets in his name. Legal precedent, however, allowed for the prosecution of people whose extravagant lifestyles had no visible means of legal support. It also permitted the government to seize anything of value that might be used to repay the tax debt. This gave Ness and his men their most powerful ammunition – authorization from the highest level to shut down and seize the mobster's breweries.

On March 13, 1931, a federal grand jury met secretly and returned an indictment in support of the government's claim that Capone had a tax liability of approximately $200,000. A quick trial found Capone guilty, fined him $50,000 and sentenced the most powerful gangster in America to eleven years in jail.

Given the probability that Capone was responsible for more than 100 murders, his sentence may not seem overly harsh. Nevertheless, Capone never regained his stature of mob leader and died after spending hard time in Alcatraz.

Now, that I have laid the groundwork on tax evasion, let's talk about legitimate tax incentives that moviemakers can use to lower their taxable income on their projects.

Many states offer tax incentives to lure TV and film producers to shoot in their states. The incentives are usually designed to attract top talent who can bring buzz to the local economy. In many cases, the incentives are tied to hiring local people, thus creating jobs, which politicians can talk about with the Press and their voting constituents.

After years of observing the effects of successful foreign film and television-production tax incentives, the United States amended its views and tax policy to counteract the effects of runaway production (i.e., US film production in Canada attracted by Canadian tax incentives).

This change of position by the federal government was evidenced by a number of states' production tax incentive programs, such as Hawaii's Investment Tax Credit, New Mexico's Film Production Tax Credit and its Filmmaker Gross Receipts Tax Reduction and Missouri's Film Production Tax Credit.

However, since it is fairly easily to justify tax incentives, experts now estimate that more than 40 states now offer different forms of tax incentives. It is my experience that many of these incentives are worthless to independent filmmakers because large studios with lots of money tend to grab most of them to lower their overall production. In particular, the paperwork is not easy to complete and most states shut down the credits when they run out of money, especially in this tough economy.

For example, let's talk about New York.

The four major television networks unveiled nearly 40 new shows for the coming season during the annual upfront dog-and-pony show in May 2010. But so far, only one of them, Tom Selleck's police drama, Blue Bloods, is set to be filmed in New York.

Executives at the city's sound stages, where the shows are filmed, are still scrambling to land new programs, but that effort is being severely hobbled, they complain, by the lack of a crucial state tax incentives that production companies depend on to lower the cost of working in New York City.

The state's hugely popular tax incentive program, which offers a 30% credit on production expenditures if a number of stipulations are met, ran out of money more than a year ago. It was then extended for just 12 months and is now up for renewal. In his most recent budget proposal, Gov. David Paterson included $420 million for the film tax credit and extended the program through 2014. Film executives, who have been lobbying relentlessly, are confident the measure will be signed into law. But with the state's budget already two months late and no sign of an end to the legislative paralysis in Albany, that extension may come too late.

At this point, industry executives say that the uncertainty over the tax incentive program has all but wiped out New York's pilot business this year. In contrast, just two years ago, the city attracted a record 21 pilots, some of which went on to some level of success as a series.

This year's new-series drought comes as the industry is reeling from the May 13 cancellation of its long-running cash cow, Law & Order. According to the Mayor's Office of Film, Theater and Broadcasting, the series pumped $79 million into the local economy annually. Over the course of its 20-year run, the show spent an estimated $1 billion.

What about Pennsylvania? M. Night Shyamalan's latest film production, "The Last Airbender," was recently awarded over $35 million in film tax credits from Pennsylvania over a two-year production period. The award is the largest in the history of Pennsylvania's Film Tax Credit (FTC), breaking the record held by his previous project, "The Happening," which received $12 million in tax credits. His film "Lady in the Water" also received a film production grant.

Pennsylvania is among the 26 of 44 states that offer transferable (or in some states refundable) tax credits to film producers. This means that if the tax credit awarded are more than the actual state taxes the recipient owes, they can sell the remaining credit to another business.

In my home state of Arizona, the tax credits are a joke. A film industry tax incentive that rewards companies for filming in Arizona expired at the end of 2010. One of the local communities, Avondale, fears that the loss of the tax credit could kill a $100 million television and movie studio project, called Avondale Live, and thousands of potential jobs.

The lapsing of the tax incentive also could affect plans for Gateway Studios, a $70 million production-studio complex in Mesa.

Sen. John Nelson, a Litchfield Park Republican, sponsored the bill. He worries Arizona may be on the verge of killing an entire industry in the state, citing that New Mexico, Louisiana and Michigan are aggressively courting the industry.

Not everyone is enamored of the tax credit, though. It was a fight getting the bill out of the Arizona state Senate, with some legislators saying they couldn't justify giving out tax credits to the film industry while making steep cuts in education and health services. Some complained the tax credits favored one industry over others.

Why don't film tax incentives "create jobs"? In part, they provide incentives for economic activity that would have occurred anyway. Furthermore, a narrow tax incentive does little to improve the overall economy. Indeed, the tax breaks given to the film industry could instead have been used to lower taxes on all businesses, rewarding entrepreneurship rather than lobbying.

While film production tax credits remain popular, as lawmakers love the chance to have movie stars show up in their districts, many states are reconsidering their benefits. Wisconsin Gov. Jim Doyle pushed for elimination of his state's film tax credit. Iowa's film tax credit was recently suspended, and criminal charges were filed for "stealing" tax credits when filmmakers inflated costs and took the tax credit while actually filming and hiring workers in other states.

Here is a brief list of state tax incentives. Since they change frequently, you will need to visit the various state tax websites to get current information:

Arizona – as far as I am concerned, my new home state (I used to live in New York, California, Utah and North Carolina) has blown it with their state tax incentives. The legislature is parochial and does not understand the creative needs of the entertainment industry. Regardless of what you may think about tax incentives, Arizona is a beautiful place with three distinct sceneries (Flagstaff to the North, Phoenix in the middle and Tucson to the South) and a group of very talented moviemakers who previously worked in major motion picture centers and came to Arizona for a better lifestyle.

Rather than centralizing tax incentive information, the state allows various areas (Phoenix, Yuma, Sedona and others) to set up offices. I believe that this type of decentralization tells moviemakers that they have to work too hard and jump through too many hoops to get accurate and current information throughout the State.

The primary goal of the Motion Picture Production Tax Incentives Program is to promote and stimulate the production of commercial motion pictures in Arizona. The program achieves this goal by providing incentives to qualified companies that produce motion pictures in Arizona and to persons who construct infrastructure projects in Arizona.

California - The California Film Commission (CFC) monitors the most recent tax incentives passed in May 2010. Due to pent-up demand, the program was fully subscribed immediately for fiscal 2010. The CFC maintains a waiting list for projects that wish to apply for future fiscals.

Qualified taxpayers are allowed a credit against income and/or sales and use taxes, based on qualified expenditures, for taxable years beginning on or after January 1, 2011. Credits applied to income tax liability are not refundable. Only tax credits issued to an "independent film" may be transferred or sold to an unrelated party. Other qualified taxpayers may carryover tax credits for 5 years and transfer tax credits to an affiliate.

Feature Films ($1 million minimum - $75 million maximum production budget) are eligible for a 20% tax credit. An "independent film", with budgets between $1 million - $10 million that is produced by a company that is not publicly traded is eligible for a 25% tax credit on more than 75% of production days or total production budget in California.

Meanwhile, California, the traditional epicenter of the US film industry, has declined to enact tax incentives, a contentious issue that has come before the state legislature numerous times. It's unlikely that California, in the midst of a budget crisis, will this year pass a bill to compete with places like Michigan or New Mexico.

Louisiana – Louisiana has been at the forefront of attracting moviemakers to the state. In 2006, they created strong tax incentives in order to offset the devastating effects of Hurricane Katrina. To this day, they still talk about their motives for creating the incentives.

As of the beginning of 2006, Louisiana passed a newly amended transferable investment tax credit of 25% on qualified expenditures grants taxpayers domiciled in Louisiana against state income tax if their total base investment is greater than three-hundred thousand dollars ($300,000).

Fundamentally, the Louisiana government gives a transferable tax credit to production companies for shooting in the state. The credit is salable to taxpayers, which predominantly include Louisiana-based companies that can use the credit on their own expenditures. Research indicates that taxpayers often are able to buy the credit at a discount.

Massachusetts - The state of Massachusetts has a Film Production Tax Credit (FPTC) equal to 25% of in-state production costs (not including payroll expenses used to claim the payroll credit), if 50% of the total expenses or production time are spent within the state. The tax credit requires a $50,000 minimum spend in the state to order to qualify for the entire incentive.

Michigan - In early 2009, Michigan Gov. Jennifer Granholm announced the development of a new $54 million movie production facility to be built in Pontiac as part of an ambitious and costly plan to build a film business amid the ashes of the auto industry.

The studio — to be built in a shuttered General Motors facility — is expected to create about 3,600 new jobs, marking one of the most audacious attempts by a state to attract new industries by offering generous tax incentives.

Michigan began offering tax incentives several years ago to lure filmmakers away from Hollywood. But since then, competition has increased from New Mexico, Louisiana, Rhode Island and Georgia, which offer skilled workers with production and post-production facilities; not to mention a more aesthetically appealing environment.

This rabid tax legislation competition has forced states like Michigan to try to find ways to sweeten the pot to maintain momentum in its efforts to build up an industry from scratch. The state isn't contributing cash for the facility's construction. But it is offering $15 million in film-related tax credits, plus as much as $101 million in state tax credits over 12 years, if hiring goals are met.

Michigan's efforts to lure film production have shown mixed results so far, despite such aggressive incentives as a law signed last year that offers cash refunds of 40% or more to productions that spend more than $50,000 in state. Hollywood studios have moved some individual productions to the state, such as the Clint Eastwood hit "Gran Torino," which Warner Bros. shifted to the Detroit area from Minnesota to take advantage of the rebates.

There's a lot of news right now about a purported 3,500 new movie industry jobs that could be on their way to metro Detroit. The jobs are attributed to the state government's generous film incentive program. The program is the state's marquee response to a prolonged economic malaise, in which the state has lost more than a half million jobs since the year 2000.

Montana - the State offers a tax rebate on hired Montana labor, 9% Tax rebate on qualified expenditures (rentals, food, lodging) with no minimum spend or cap and no sales tax

Out-of-state equipment used exclusively in film production is exempt from property tax for 180 consecutive days.

New Mexico — offers a 25% Tax Rebate with no minimum budget requirement, no minimum spend requirement, no minimum shoot day requirement and no minimum resident hire requirement with no caps.

New York — The New York City "Made in NY" Film Production Tax Credit program provides qualifying film and television productions a fully refundable tax credit equal to 5% of qualified production expenditures. New York State offers a separate, but similar program, which provides qualifying film and television productions a 30% credit, for a total tax credit equal to 35% of qualified production expenditures.

Eligible productions include Feature Films, Television series, pilots, movies and miniseries

For a feature film or television project to be eligible for the credit, the production must first:

1) build a set and shoot at least one day on a stage at a qualified production facility

2) complete at least 75% of the total facility-related expenses at a qualified facility

Once the stage requirement is met, the costs of location work, post-production, and other work done in New York, but outside the facility, are eligible if at least 75% of the location shooting days are in New York. If the production spends at least $3 million on work incurred at the qualified facility, the location threshold is waived.

Ohio – In July, 2009, Governor Ted Strickland signed into law Ohio budget bill (HB 1) including Sec. 122.85, which creates a Film Tax Credit for Ohio. The bill provides for a refundable credit against the corporation franchise or income tax for motion pictures produced in Ohio.

The tax credit is equal to 25 percent of non-wage and nonresident wage Ohio production expenditures and 35 percent of Ohio resident wage production expenditures.

Up to $5 million in credits is available per production. A total of $30 million in credits are available in the FY 2010-2011 budget.

Pennsylvania - Pennsylvania first created a film tax credit in 2004, replaced it with a film grant program in 2006, then enacted its current $75 million tax credit program in 2007, in which films can receive up to 25 percent of production costs in the form of a tax credit. The state's FTC was temporarily reduced, as the 2009 state budget agreement reduced all tax credits by 33% for three years.

Out-of-Country - Of course, the most adventurous moviemakers head out of the country to make their films.

The British Columbia Production Services Tax Credit (PSTC) encourages film, television and animation production in BC and is available to either international or Canadian productions produced in British Columbia. The Canadian Federal Government's Film or Video Production Services Tax Credit (PSTC) is primarily for foreign production and is 16% of Canadian labor costs.

There are four components:

1. The basic PSTC tax credit is 33% of qualified BC labor expenditures incurred after February 28, 2010.

2. The Regional tax credit is 6% of qualified BC labor expenditures of the corporation pro-rated the number of days of principal photography in BC outside of the designated Vancouver area to the total days of principal photography in BC.

3. The new Distant Location tax credit is 6% and is added to the regional tax credit for principal photography done outside of the Lower Mainland Region, north of Whistler and east of Hope, excluding the Capital Regional District.

4. Digital Animation or Visual Effects tax credit is 17.5% of BC labor expenditures directly attributable to digital animation or visual effects activities.

Movie incentives by-and-large have failed as economic policy. Movie production incentives are costly and fail to live up to their promises. Among these failures, the two most important are their failure to encourage economic growth overall and their failure to raise tax revenue.

The bottom line is that tax incentives are knee-jerk reactions by state legislators enamored by Hollywood and the seduction by the rich, famous, beautiful and reckless. They rush to offer tax breaks and other incentives to film production companies that create jobs. States, who have examined hefty tax breaks for film and television production, conclude that they are not a good idea in a recession and that they cost states more money than they generate.

Chapter 18
"The Internet Threat"

In 1948, when only one in ten Americans had seen a television set made by RCA, TIME magazine sized up the new medium. "Its quiz shows, cooking lessons and vaudeville performances were perfectly watchable," it said, "but the films were awful." "The ancient cabbages that are rolled across the telescreen every night are Hollywood's curse on the upstart industry," it wrote. "Televiewers, sick of hoary Hoot Gibson oaters and antique spook comedies, wonder when, if ever, they will see fresh, first-class Hollywood films."

Sixty years have not done much to alter Tinseltown's instincts. As it prepares for its future, Hollywood faces another new medium—the Internet. Instead of using the web to get films to people, Studios still have not been able to figure it out. If the Studios hope that by ignoring the web, Tinseltown can put off (or at least control and manipulate) change, they are surely wrong. Hollywood needs to confront the web by embracing it.

In the 1940s, Studios feared TV because they thought it would destroy movie theaters. Now, they believe that the Internet will spoil sales of DVDs, which in America now bring in about half of their total revenues. In fact, DVD sales have continued to plummet in the aftermath of the Great Recession, and with the loss of Walmart and Blockbuster buying films, many are depending on Netflix and Hulu to kick 'streaming' sales.

Meanwhile, box-office revenues are flat and Cable TV now rivals Hollywood productions with premium acting talent, dynamic stories and top directing talent.

As revenue projections look weaker, production and marketing costs have spiraled appallingly and obscenely upwards. When a film brings in more than $100 million, Will Smith and Johnny Depp can get $20m upfront and then 20% of gross receipts. This sad state of affairs cannot last.

At Disney, such payments and various add-ons have more than tripled in the past four years. With more money going to writers, actors and directors, there is less money available to producers and investors.

In light of these circumstances, you would think the Studios would be falling over themselves to find new sources of online revenue. The success of a film like "Cloverfield," which found its audience through marketing almost entirely on the internet, points to how the Hollywood core audience —teenagers and young adults—is fascinated by all things web-related. In private, even Hollywood studio executives admit that their children don't buy CDs or DVDs. They go on the Internet and download their favorite movie.

Although the studios spend millions on websites to advertise every film, no major Hollywood studio sells the newest releases direct to the consumer via the web. It is partly because the DVD business relies on big retailers such as Walmart and Best Buy, who take the risk and make the money.

To keep them happy, Hollywood holds back most of its films from the web in order to get people into the retail stores. One can easily see that Hollywood has commoditized the DVDs business making them readily available in supermarkets, airports, retail stores, and video rental outlets for as cheap as $1.00/rental. Why would anyone go to a movie and pay top dollar when all they have to do is wait till the price comes down to a level they can afford?

Every time Hollywood has offered people a more convenient way to watch its films, sales have increased. Bringing movies into the home via television, VHS and DVD built the industry into what it is today.

The Internet may look unfamiliar and dangerous, but it could become the ultimate home entertainment weapon. A company like NetFlix, which sells DVDs, had a specific goal when it launched nearly 10 years ago – show flicks on the net to avoid the cost of manufacturing DVDs and renting them.

Even now, NetFlix offers the ability to stream high quality video from its site to your computer. No trip to a thinly stocked retailer, no late fees, no waiting for a package in the mail; instead, on-demand access to any film you want, from the latest blockbuster to the most obscure art-house tearjerker.

Since distribution costs are dramatically reduced, profits actually rise. The same thing is happening in the book industry with people downloading e-books onto their Kindle.

Of course, "going to the movies" and watching a great picture on a huge screen will continue. Sitting in the dark with a group of strangers and experiencing the emotional and psychological power of a superbly crafted film will continue to survive, especially as 3D technology continues to evolve.

Go to Google or Bing and type in the phrase, "movie download." You will see hundreds of sites fighting for your business. In fact, one site claims to have access to over 80 million movies online as well as access to sporting events, TV shows and podcasts.

At this rate, we will probably see the day when the only way to make money is to distribute an independent film directly to a movie enthusiast who follows you and your projects. For without a direct, human connection it is going to be extremely difficult to get your product into the hands of the buyer.

If you read as many papers and journals as I do, you get the impression that movie theaters are dead and that everyone is going to download movies from the Internet onto their favorite portable media player, whether it be a phone, computer or TV.

No one can predict the future. However, there are several veteran producers who are willing to share their viewpoints.

Excerpted comments from Hollywood trade magazines:

JONATHAN SEHRING,
IFC ENTERTAINMENT

The rise and fall of studio specialty divisions has come about because of size, ego, envy and hubris. Corporations bought the studios and a different set of economics came into play.

HOWARD COHEN,
ROADSIDE ATTRACTIONS

When Miramax was a pioneer for this type and budget of film in the '90s, the DVD gravy train of the time made them profitable. Now, they lose money more often than not. Now the only significant upside is Oscars. And in tough economic times, that just isn't enough.

True American indies have always had their ups and downs, but I would agree we're going through a fallow period where it's hard to get people to see them in theaters. Part of it is that the heavyweight casting and heavy TV marketing used on the more "midlevel" American films, such as "There Will Be Blood," have conditioned the audience in a bad way and made it harder on excellent small films like "Wendy and Lucy" and "Sugar." They look puny by comparison without all the ad dollars, fewer people see them, and they are gone from theaters quickly.

Aesthetically, I don't think anything will ever replace a 40-foot screen and a shared audience experience. My confidence in that keeps me in the theatrical game. I hope there will always be people in our society who can afford that luxury

BOB BERNEY,
APPARITION STUDIOS

Although there will be fewer ambitious films made, they will not disappear. It will be interesting to see if some of these same studios decide to return to the mid-level, auteur films in a few years, starting these divisions all over again. It's a cycle that has been repeated several times.

MICHAEL BARKER,
SONY PICTURES CLASSICS

When I started in this business over 29 years ago, there was no home entertainment to speak of and rarely, if ever, did television play independent or foreign language films. Former porno houses and bowling alleys became art theaters, and the major circuits never played an independent film of any kind. Yes, independent films always opened and did well in New York City, but quite often these films didn't go to many places west of the Hudson River. Today, we have major independent theater circuits (Landmark Theaters, Angelika theaters, the newer digital Emerging Cinemas) that have an insatiable appetite for independent films.

ADAM YAUCH,
OSCILLOSCOPE LABORATORIES

People still want to go out to the movies on a date, or as an outing with friends, and hands down it is still the best way to experience a film. There is something to be said for the whole experience, even buying a ticket, queuing up, finding your seat, the energy of an audience when they laugh or feel emotion, not to mention a big screen, a powerful sound system, a dark room, and the film playing from beginning to end without being paused to answer the door or the phone. The whole experience of going to the movies can't really be compared with watching something on your TV or phone. People have not stopped going to concerts even when they can listen to a band's CD or to a laptop or plasma screen or cell phone.

Chapter 19

Summary

So where does this leave us? I believe that the movie industry is nothing more than legalized gambling. Similar to Wall Street, it rewards those with the best connections, and has the power to make a lot of money for those who get in on the ground floor. Investors can become overnight millionaires and then bet the proceeds again on a sequel, and potentially lose everything. Actors can become famous, invest their own money in their own projects and lose everything. Producers have the unlimited opportunity to connect with the right people and wind up on the red carpet, only to fall again when their instincts lead them to believe that they can do anything. Or, they age and simply fade away.

The independent filmmaker is faced with a myriad of challenges, ranging from lack of capital and direction, unreasonable business plan assumptions, temperamental actors and directors, ever-changing technological landscapes and unpredictable weather. Coupled with extreme competition from both well-healed movie studios fighting for their survival and bright intelligent people with great ideas, the industry destroys people along the way as it rewards those who survive.

So, let's hear from some famous Hollywood personalities and their thoughts on the dream machine:

Hollywood is a place where they'll pay you a thousand dollars for a kiss and fifty cents for your soul.

Marilyn Monroe

In Hollywood, the woods are full of people that learned to write but evidently can't read. If they could read their stuff, they'd stop writing.

Will Rogers

Mickey Mouse popped out of my mind and onto a drawing pad 20 years ago on a train ride from Manhattan to Hollywood at a time when the business fortunes of my brother Roy and myself were at their lowest ebb and disaster seemed right around the corner.

Walt Disney

I love Los Angeles. I love Hollywood. They're beautiful. Everybody's plastic, but I love plastic. I want to be plastic.

Andy Warhol

I don't think the money people in Hollywood have ever thought I was normal, but I am dedicated to my work and that's what counts.

Angelina Jolie

I sure lost my musical direction in Hollywood. My songs were the same conveyer belt mass production, just like most of my movies were.

Elvis Presley

It's good to experience Hollywood in short bursts, I guess. Little snippets. I don't think I can handle being here all the time, it's pretty nutty.

Johnny Depp

Hollywood is a place where a man can get stabbed in the back while climbing a ladder.

William Faulkner

I'm not a Hollywood basher because enough good movies come out of the Hollywood system every year to justify its existence, without any apologies.

Quentin Tarantino

I think the bottom of the totem pole is African-American women, or women of color. I think they get the least opportunities in Hollywood.

Denzel Washington

Every country gets the circus it deserves. Spain gets bullfights. Italy gets the Catholic Church. America gets Hollywood.

Erica Jong

To be quite honest, I've been very blessed when I've worked with Hollywood. The studios that have purchased my work to be adapted to film have really liked the work and wanted to stay as close as they could to what the book was.

Nicholas Sparks

I always thought the real violence in Hollywood isn't what's on the screen. It's what you have to do to raise the money.

David Mamet

Hollywood people are filled with guilt: white guilt, liberal guilt, money guilt. They feel bad that they're so rich, they feel they don't work that much for all that money - and they don't, for the amount of money they make.

Drew Carey

The ladder of success in Hollywood is usually a press agent, actor, director, producer, leading man; and you are a star if you sleep with each of them in that order. Crude, but true.

Hedy Lamarr

I think Hollywood has a class system. The actors are like the inmates, but the truth is they're running the asylum.

Robert De Niro

That's the biggest rule in Hollywood: Don't spend your own money.

Pauly Shore

If only those who dream about Hollywood knew how difficult it all is.

Greta Garbo

A final comment: You are not alone in your journey to make a great independent film. There are many organizations and film festivals dedicated to helping you with your independent film project. Learn to network. Go out and meet as many people who might be able to get your project off the ground. You cannot become successful sitting behind a desk typing away at a computer. That, unfortunately, is only the first step on your tiring and uphill journey.

And, of course, I encourage you to periodically check out my website, http://showbizmanagementadvisors.com. Please feel free to download any of the information that you find posted on my website. It is free and I provide it from my heart to those who strive to become the next generation of independent filmmakers.

Good luck and may God Bless.

www.ingramcontent.com/pod-product-compliance
Lightning Source LLC
Chambersburg PA
CBHW071420160426
43195CB00013B/1760